20

San Francisco's
GOLDEN ERA

San Francisco's
GOLDEN ERA

A Picture Story of San Francisco Before The Fire

By Lucius Beebe
& Charles Clegg

Howell-North • Berkeley, California • 1960

THE FRONTISPIECE

Fireman's Fund Insurance Co., Collection

The painting on which the frontispiece is based is the work of the brothers Charles and Arthur Nahl, two of California's foremost pictorial artists of the nineteenth century and is from the collection of the Fireman's Fund. It depicts a scene in San Francisco harbor on July 24, 1853 when fire broke out among the hulks of sailing ships deserted by their crews for the gold fields. The town's primeval fire companies are depicted being rowed out to the scene of conflagration from the waterfront and engaging in spirited battle with the flames while onlookers cheer from every available vantage point. The original sketch of the event from which the Nahls worked was made by an eyewitness, a delivery boy in the service of Edward T. Batturs, a grocer with a shop on Grant Avenue, who drew the fire as he saw it on a boxtop. The painting, which was for many years in the Batturs family before being acquired by the Fireman's Fund, in addition to its obvious animation and excitement, is interesting for showing in the background the newly completed outline of the Marine Hospital on Rincon Hill.

SAN FRANCISCO'S GOLDEN ERA

Printed and bound in the United States of America.

Library of Congress Catalogue Card No. 60-15642

First Printing September, 1960

Second Printing October, 1960

Published by Howell-North Books

1050 Parker Street, Berkeley 10, California

ACKNOWLEDGEMENTS

For many good and kind offices of scholarship and assistance in the assembl-
ing of this nosegay of times past the authors want to thank Donald Biggs
and James deT. Abajian of the California Historical Society; Dr. George P.
Hammond, Dr. John Barr Tompkins and Dr. James S. Holliday of the Bancroft Library, University of California at Berkeley; Dr. Elliott Evans and
Mrs. Hester Robinson of the Society of California Pioneers; Miss Irene
Simpson of the Wells Fargo History Room; Dr. Albert Shumate, the officers
of the Fireman's Fund Insurance Company, William Bronson and the
Oakland Art Museum for generous pictorial loans, and finally that venerable
custodian of San Francisco yesterdays, Roy D. Graves. Without their interest and great courtesy, this book for whatever modest worth it may
assume, would not have been thinkable, and to them it is dedicated in
gratitude.

CONTENTS

FOREWORD

An established, if altogether mendacious theory, has for some years been advocated as a tenet of the American credo to the effect that what passes for love is everything. It has been the continuing theme of literature, the stage and later films and, one may suppose, television. Love is eternal. Love or perish. It's love that makes the world go round. The love of a brave man for a good woman has been held up as the summum bonum of terrestrial desire, the supreme accomplishment of a universal and eternal scheme of things. Practitioners of beautiful letters have invoked the theme of togetherness and the nuptial couch as transcending all other aspects of existence.

Nothing could be more remote from the truth, at least in the American philosophy of life. The theme of success and the achievement of wealth has, from earliest times, left love at the post. It is the sudden achievement of vast and, preferably, undeserved riches that makes the American heart beat fastest of all. Diamonds have always been a girl's best friend and the Street & Smith paper back novels concerned with the achievements of The Boy Broker in Wall Street outsold all the rest, saving perhaps the national God-image of Buffalo Bill Cody.

Deplorable as it may be, America's most enduring romance has not been with the heroines of Victorian fiction, with the Gibson Girl of the turn of the century or the celluloid prostitutes who have offered themselves vicariously at a thousand cinemas. It has been with the solid and enduring female image that from time immemorial has been part of our minted coinage, the Goddess of Plenty in fancy dress makeup as Liberty that has appeared on eagles and double eagles, cartwheels, two bit pieces and dimes. The face on the dollar is the national sweetheart and only an incurable romanticist or the author of novels for the serving girl trade will contend otherwise.

This explains without any possible alternative why San Francisco has always been the American dream image of a city. There are other contributing factors, the greatest of which is that San Francisco is the quintessence of The West. "Make no mistake, stranger," Bernard De Voto has said, "San Francisco is West as all hell." It is this Western character that has, in part, endeared the town to successive generations of perceptive people and inspired a now forgotten prize fighter named Willie Britt to declare: "I'd rather be a busted lamp post in Battery Street than the Waldorf Astoria."

There are other lesser considerations of meteorology, of space and sky and climate, the things that moved Joaquin Miller to write:

"Such room to live; such room to die!
Such room to live in after death!"

and there are factors of employment, esthetics and domestic economy. All of these contribute to the essential character of what Hubert Howe Bancroft, with no inhibitions at all about the superlative, called simply "The center of the earth."

But San Francisco's everlasting appeal to all Americans and to such foreigners as are gifted with direct vision and no nonsense is that it is a city that smells of money. Herb Caen, the town's poet laureate of the twentieth century, makes a good thing out of its other smells: roasting coffee, fog, fried fish and a variety of olfactory endearments. But the smell San Franciscans have always recognized as most compelling has been that native to Montgomery Street, to the town's swaggering banks and to its United States Mint.

In this it has enjoyed a clear and unmistakable vote of confidence from the rest of the country.

San Franciscans have always recognized that love had little to do with making the mare go. It was scratch or wampum, and the town has for decades admired fast horses.

San Francisco, since the earliest years of the American occupancy, has always been a money town. When John Jacob Astor was clipping dimes in the trade in New York real estate and Commodore Vanderbilt was ferrying passengers to Staten Island for a shilling, the wife of San Francisco's Mayor William K. Garrison was pouring tea from a solid gold service, the first such in America, and J. W. Tucker, the town's first jeweler, was advertising silver watches that weighed a full, honest pound, "since no miner could be found who would carry one that weighed less." While New York's richest man and most celebrated curmudgeon, A. T. Stewart, was sweating the clerks in his department store at an average salary of $5.00 a week, San Franciscans were falling over each other to subscribe $5.00 a seat for concert hall seats to hear Ostinelli, an Italian violinist.

By the time, a couple of decades later, that August Belmont, William H. Vanderbilt and other Fifth Avenue magnificoes were bugging the eyes of the peasants with English butlers, imitation French chateaux designed by Richard Hunt and seagoing yachts with genuine Brussels carpets, San Francisco was way out front with tackrooms full of silver harness for its blooded horses, twenty course public dinners off gold plate at the Palace Hotel and private balls at Burlingame to which guests were transported by special trains of parlor cars running on the hour every hour all night long, both ways.

With a population that never, until well into the current century, approached the million mark, San Francisco was a participant in recurrent and indeed almost continuous bonanzas that permitted money, which naturally first accrued at the top of the pile, to filter down to the lower strata of its inhabitants to a degree unknown and almost unbelievable in less favored communities. The community as a whole was well-to-do. The nabobs were simply rolling in it.

The first and most celebrated source of San Francisco wealth was, of course, the gold of the Mother Lode which was uncovered in the Sierra foothills in 1858 and by the following year had precipitated the California gold rush that marked the high water tide of easy wealth to date, settled the American West and lent validity to the all-embracing doctrine of Manifest Destiny. With Sacramento as its entrepot, the gold of Hangtown, Negro Bar, Fiddle Town, Gold Run and Amador was almost without the divergence of an ounce, funnelled through San Francisco aboard the Concord coaches and in the green painted treasure chests of Wells Fargo, the princely bankers and express forwarders of Montgomery Street.

In what other city in the world would there have been built commercial office premises whose masonry would be precious enough to encourage its theft? Yet when the Virginia City bonanza kings opened their own Nevada Bank at the corner of Pine and Montgomery with a capitalization of $10,000,000.00, the largest in the world at the time, its overmantles in various offices designed for rent were of gold bearing quartz from the deep mines of the Comstock. An early tenant departed one night having unseated the overmantle in his office and broken it up for handy removal and the eventual recovery of its precious metal content.

When the Mother Lode began to run thin, a second suburb of Golconda was unearthed under Virginia City in the Washoe Hills of the Nevada desert. The mines and mills of the Comstock Lode, owned, managed and directed out of San Francisco, first by the all-powerful Bank of California and later by the bonanza firm of Flood, Fair, Mackay and O'Brien, in four decades produced well over a half billion in gold and silver bullion, every smidgen of which went across the Sierra to the counting houses and vaults of San Francisco.

Coincidental with the decline of the Mother Lode and the rise of the Comstock, the Pacific Railroad was completed, the western portion by California capitalists who had started laying track in a modest way out of Sacramento and ended as figures of such towering wealth and power that for a full generation the entire state of California was no more than their feudal property, its inhabitants held in fief, its land in fee simple.

An interesting footnote to the dimensions of the fortunes deriving from the Southern Pacific is that after the death of the richest of the partners, his widow Arabella Huntington absentmindedly forgot when leaving the premises of a Fifth Avenue art dealer her handbag containing eleven pearl necklaces valued at $3,555,000. She explained the lapse by saying she had something else on her mind. Also, that when Huntington's nephew and heir, Henry E. Huntington, wished to purchase from an English ducal family Gainsborough's finest and most famous painting, "The Blue Boy," he was momentarily embarrassed for cash and had to ask for twenty-four hours in which to lay hands on $620,000.

And during the exploration and enjoyment of these incredible bonanzas San Francisco banked the untold riches deriving from such ocean shipping firms as the Pacific Mail Steamship Company which plied the ocean lanes between "the states" and California, at first around Cape Horn, then via the Isthmus of Panama and eventually extended sea lanes out of San Francisco all over the Pacific. The Panama steamers in conjunction with the Panama Railroad made a score of millionaires, including Trenor Park and others whose names have become lost in the roll call of richer men that engulfed them. An entire monograph of substantial proportions could be written about San Francisco's men of great wealth whose names, in so far as posterity is concerned, were submerged in the mob of rich millionaires around them: Park, Alvinza Hayward, "a picturesque figure of elegant manners and sulphuric profanity who struck it rich on Sutter's Creek"; bearded old Ben Holladay, the staging king; Alvin Adams, the expressing magnate who was eventually overwhelmed by Wells Fargo & Co.; the cattle kings Miller and Lux; and Michael Reese, the real estate broker.

In any American community of ordinarily abundant life in the mid-nineteenth century these would have stood out as the collective Medicis and Rothschilds of the countryside. In San Francisco their names are forgotten save by professional social historians.

Thomas Carlyle's classic definition of respectability was "a man who kept a gig," but long before the Civil War hundreds of San Franciscans had achieved greater respectability with broughams, landaus, victorias, surreys and dog carts. The *grand-daumont-de-visite* of Newport which was guided by postillions with footmen up behind, never gained a foothold on Nob Hill, but there were English drags in the grand manner for coaching to the Seal Rocks for Sunday breakfast and James C. Flood's town carriages and opera coaches were the envy of visiting royalty.

As a natural consequence of the gold that flowed in seemingly inexhaustible torrents from the surface diggings of the Mother Lode, gold at an early stage in the game became the property most closely associated with San Francisco as well as its only recognized currency. Private mints turned out fifty dollar octagonal slugs and twenty dollar double eagles before there was an official United States Mint in California. The first primeval hallmark of success in the shack town of San Francisco was the nugget watch chain sported by newly rich miners sweeping in aureate cable lengths across brocaded waistcoats. The first practical joke of record that provoked roars of mirth in early San Franciscans was when a group of young bloods "salted" Sacramento Street with $2,000 worth of gold dust and nuggets for which gullible Easterners from a newly docked passenger packet clawed and fought when they left the gangway.

The town's first literary paper of consequence was called *The Golden Era;* when the rails of the Pacific Railroad were joined at Promontory in Utah in 1869 a spike of pure California gold was driven and the original can be seen in Wells Fargo's museum to this day. Women of fashion at one period sprinkled gold flakes in their hair as a footman would do with powder, and gold coin was the only medium of exchange permitted on the tables of gambling layouts in Portsmouth Square. Before the phrase "Diamond Horseshoe" was coined at New York's Metropolitan, the dress circle at the opera was known in San Francisco as The Golden Horseshoe.

When seventeen-year-old Mike de Young borrowed twenty dollars from his landlord to start what is today's *Chronicle* it was in the form of a double eagle and it was stipulated to be returned in the same form. Gold service plates and flat silver became commonplace on Nob Hill and James Ben Ali Haggin had an entire extra such service made by Shreve for his private Pullman car *Salvator*. When the *San Francisco Call* was up for sale before the Master in Chancery, Delmas Demas, attorney for a prospective purchaser, appeared in court flanked by five men with wicker market baskets containing $25,000 in gold as a deposit.

Such an abundance of the metal that in all ages has not only symbolized wealth but itself been wealth tangible and concrete, did nothing to abate San Francisco's reputation as the richest and most desirable of American cities.

Even the servants in early San Francisco partook of the general well-being. Jesse Benton Fremont lost a chambermaid when she was refused the loan of her employer's evening dresses to be copied by a Chinese couturier. Maud Wilkinson Richardson, granddaughter of a Forty-niner, used to recall how her grandmother's washerwoman on arriving on washday would unclasp a shawl "fastened with a scintillant diamond brooch worthy of an Empress."

San Franciscans began living high on the hog in a matter of weeks after Sam Brannan, the town's first booster and high pressure operator generally had broadcast the tidings of gold on the American River. They began ordering fancy comestibles in shipload quantities and paying top prices for champagne and Madeira, New England butter, Maryland terrapin and other concentrated calories and taking three hours for lunch, amiable habits that haven't entirely disappeared to this day. As this article is being written the City of Paris, one of the better known department stores of the town, is advertising "Come In and See Our $10,000.00 Display of Alsace Lorraine Pate de Foie Gras With Truffles." It is safe to say that few department stores elsewhere in the land carry any such stock of foie gras or advertise the commodity in the public prints.

Restaurateurs all over the world and French chefs of note got the news early and swarmed down the gangplanks, resolved to get in on the ground floor in a city where miners paid in gold and seldom asked for change if the souffle had been to their liking. They were, furthermore, customers to warm the heart of a *saucier* or *gard manger* fresh from Paris. Many red shirted miners with Yuba River mud on their boots were men of education and not dismayed by exotic fare or restaurant French. All of them had wonderful appetites.

An habitual diner out, a San Franciscan of the fifties admired rich decor as he admired rich sauces. Winn's Fountain Head, one of the earliest restaurants, advertised "fine venison steaks, oysters, ducks, geese, partridges, snipe and teal" in a premises characterized by "rich Turkey carpets, costly draperies, rosewood chairs with crimson velvet cushions, sofas and Italian marble tables." A contemporary advertisement for a downtown shop listed Colt's Patent revolvers at $30 to $40 a piece, Sazerac brandy, fine French champagne and "white kid gloves of superior quality at $1-1/2 the pair." The San Francisco boulevardier who packed a Colt wore white kid gloves to avoid powder burns.

But wealth didn't really begin to get in its licks until the almost simultaneous arrival early in the seventies of the bonanza kings from the Comstock and the group that has always been known as The Big Four of the Central Pacific Railroad.

Keeping up with the Joneses who were in fact the Crockers and Tevises and Haggins meant spending $3,000,000 for a town house as the merest whim, and it must be remembered that the dollar in this halcyon time bought anywhere from five to ten times what it does today.

Greatest of the magnificoes of his time was William C. Ralston whose estate at Belmont has never been appraised in dollars but which was admittedly the most princely mansion and grounds in the United States when it was opened for the entertainment of Ralston's friends. It had an air conditioning plant some seventy years before its time, its own gas works and water works to activate fountains that compared favorably with those at Versailles, and a formidable entrance gate of gilded bronze which anticipated the electric eye of today by rising when a coach drove over a concealed mechanism in the road. Dinner for 200 off silver or gold services as the spirit moved the owner, was a commonplace; there was a chef ravished from Foyot's in Paris, and stables that would have aroused envy in Napoleon III who was inordinately fond of horse flesh. When he drove home from the Bank of California in the afternoon, there were changes of horses at five private post houses along the Camino and Ralston prided himself on beating the train.

Ralston's successor was William Sharon, one time manager of the Bank of California's Virginia City branch and a man who, avid of the toga, spent better than $1,000,000 getting himself elected to the United States Senate. Sharon's San Francisco town house on Nob Hill possessed an hydraulic elevator, the first in a private home in the West and the drapes, curtains and lambrequins cost $2,000 for every window in the house. Pillow cases were supplied in each of the twenty bedrooms at a cost of $140 a pair and the console mirror on Mrs. Sharon's dressing table set the Senator back $5,000. When Sharon's daughter Flora married Sir Thomas George Fermor-Hesketh, seventh Baronet, the newspapers reported that champagne flowed quite literally in rivers and that the Senator had settled on his daughter the same sum William H. Vanderbilt had given as dowry when Consuelo married the Duke of Marlborough, $2,500,000. This was merely for pocket money as, contrary to the general rule, Fermor-Hesketh was well off himself.

To meet the standards set by directors of the Bank of California, Charles Crocker, one of the four rajahs of the Central Pacific Railroad, ran up a $2,300,000 home on Nob Hill and his partner, Mark Hopkins topped this with a $3,000,000 residence where the Mark Hopkins Hotel stands today. The figures are those of Julia Cooley Altrocchi, the official and enchantingly readable chronicler of San Francisco's golden era. At San Mateo Alvinza Hayward carried hippophilia to its logical conclusion by building stables that were more magnificent than his own dwelling. The stables were lit by municipal gas, there were mosaic floors, redwood and mahogany stalls, a plate glass harness room and silver mounted harnesses. In the tack room was a crystal chandelier from the palace of a Venetian doge.

The stables of James Ben Ali Haggin, handy to the Nob Hill palace of the Wells Fargo magnate and mining partner of Senator George Hearst, were so handsomely appointed that visitors to San Francisco asked to be conducted through them as they would through a public museum or other attraction and the horse breeder, who also owned immense stables at Sacramento, in Fayette County near Lexington, Kentucky, and eventually purchased the Whitney stables near Sheepshead Bay in New York, liked to entertain distinguished guests there much as he would in his own palatial dining room. As a fitting finale to such splendors, Haggin had a number of guests in for supper with the horses after the opera the last evening before the fire in 1906 and the footmen were still clearing the table at five in the morning when the crack of doom sounded.

In 1877 a commentator wrote in the *Argonaut*: "When a San Franciscan gets to be immensely wealthy he builds a palace of a stable with marble halls, Brussels carpet and hot and cold water in every stall; a Chicago millionaire builds a college."

In most of the proper Nob Hill houses the carpets were supplied by John Sloane, a furniture dealer from New York whom Senator Sharon had commissioned to carpet the Palace Hotel when it was first built. So rich were the pickings and so many square miles of Axminsters and Wiltons were incidentally sold to San Francisco millionaires that Sloane opened a permanent branch which has been here ever since.

The final capstone of grandeur was added to the very tip-top of Nob Hill by James C. Flood, formerly a partner in the Auction Lunch Saloon, who shared in the Comstock bonanzas of Fair and Mackay when Consolidated Virginia and California mines brought in $300,000,000 inside six years. To remind himself of his saloon-keeping days, Flood, a happy Irishman not without humor, surrounded his huge brownstone mansion that is to-day the Pacific Union Club with a massive bronze fence reminiscent of a bar rail. The fence cost $50,000.

In a generation that gloried in ostentatious good living, the nabobs were not the sort to neglect the opportunities offered by the haute cuisine for gratifying at once their love of elegance and the inner man. Early in gold rush times the incomparable Francois Pioche had imported not one or two, but half a ship's passenger list of French chefs from Paris in order that the tradition of *la cuisine Francaise* might be established at the Golden Gate, and the completion of the magnificent Palace furnished a premises suitable for its most elaborate consummation.

Even in an age of ornate dining, attention was attracted by a modest collation run up at the Palace in February 1876 in honor of the by now Senator William Sharon by a group of friends. Cynical awareness of Sharon's personal character might suggest that the bill was cuffed by nobody but the Senator himself, but in any event the dinner was an eye popper, and it lost nothing in the telling in next week's edition of *Frank Leslie's Illustrated Newspaper.*

It was most emphatically a dinner to millionaires (said *Leslie's* at the outset in order that there might be no misunderstanding). The banquet hall for the occasion was located in a large suite of rooms 378, 379, 380 and 381 on the first floor at the corner of Jessie and Annie Streets. When the banquet was in progress the scene was one of rare splendor. The hand of the florist had transformed the apartment into a grotto of fairyland. Upon the bright cloth were arranged flowers in reckless profusion, while, mingling with fruit, flowers and wondrous dishes, the bright silverware glittered in the light of numerous gas jets and the set rays of sixty-four wax candles rising from radiant candelabra. The recesses formed by the bow windows were turned into beautiful conservatories, and a delicious effect was achieved by placing large mirrors against the windows as a background for the plants. The reflection of the foliage in the windows appeared to the eye as so many entrances to green houses of great depth, thus imparting the borrowed enchantment of great distances to the view. In one window was a little grove of orange trees and banana plants, another was a miniature forest of tropic palms bending gracefully to the carpet, while still a third recess was filled with ferns of every description enrapturing the vision. The walls were hung with paintings of figures and landscapes, while eighteen cages were filled with golden feathered songsters. It was in such an apartment that Mr. Sharon's "old friends of the Comstock Lode" broke bread with him that February night.

Each gentleman seated around the festive board found near his napkin a bill of fare engraved upon a plate of solid silver dug from the Comstock Lode and highly polished. These were gotten up in artistic style at a cost of forty dollars each. An elegant border was engraved on each side of the plate, enclosing the reading matter. On the front of the plate the following words were inscribed in ornamental text and script:

Dinner
to
Hon. William Sharon,
by his
Old Friends
of the
Comstock Lode.
Palace Hotel,
Feb. 8th, 1876.   San Francisco

On the reverse side was executed the following:

Menu
Huitres.
Chablis.
Consommé Royal.
Sherry, Isabella.
Saumon glacé au four à la Chambord.
Sauterne.
Boudin blanc à la Richelieu.
Château la Tour.
Filet de Boeuf à la Providence.
Champagne.
Pâté de Fois Gras.
Château Yquem.
Timbale de Volaille Americaine au Sénateur.
Clos Vougeot.
Cotélettes d'Agneau sauté au pointes d'Asperges
Sorbet.
Becassines au Cresson.
Château Margeaux.
Salade à la Française.
Dessert.

While the edibles and wines were disappearing, a string band under direction
of Professor Schlott played a delightful selection of music in an adjoining apartment, and within earshot of the opulent epicures. It was a very enjoyable affair
for those who participated in it, and many complimentary speeches were made
during the evening. The company did not disperse until a late hour, each one
taking home with him his silver bill of fare as a souvenir.

A few years after this dazzling event San Francisco was still so self-sufficient, gastro-
nomically speaking, that it was able to take a humorous view of the arrangements made
for his personal comfort during a visit from the great J. P. Morgan himself. Morgan arrived
aboard a five car private train to attend a convocation of Anglican bishops and brought
along Louis Sherry in the capacity of personal steward to serve his table in the absence of
any dependable social order west of Omaha. San Francisco was politely amused and
Charlie Crocker's chef at his Nob Hill home introduced Sherry to roulade of sand dabs.

It has been argued by subsequent commentators and moralists that the ostentation of
riches implicit in such gestures as were dear to the hearts of San Franciscans in their
golden noontide of affluence was barbarous and in the worst possible taste. Often enough
this sanctimoniousness in a later generation is nothing more than undefiled envy. "Do not
fail to speak scornfully of the Victorian Age," says J. M. Barrie. "There will be a time for
meekness when you try to better it."

The thing that is important is that fun with money in nineteenth century San Francisco was generally regarded with approval and admiration and the same is true of the
United States in general. There was no guilt attached to expensive ways and, if in the light
of subsequent and more austere standards, some of the taste involved was deplorable,
it was at worst an innocent barbarism.

People who admired to live well and could contrive to do so had no guilt fixations
about it. A generation that didn't know how happy and fortunate it was had never heard
of either psychologists or social consciousness. Money was, as Gene Fowler said some

years later, something to be thrown off the rear platforms of trains. Them as had 'em, wore 'em.

San Francisco in the years before the fire provided a sort of Big Rock Candy Mountain for the entire American people. The face of the nation was turned toward the gold fields in eagerness and delight and few men could imagine making great sums of money without the natural consequence of spending it. Good Americans when they died might, in the terms of the epigram, go to Paris. While they were alive they wanted to go to California. Oceans of champagne, silk hats and frock coats, blooded horses and houses on Nob Hill, these were the rewards that came to the industrious, the far sighted or the merely fortunate. What better scheme of things, at least on this side of the river could any man ask?

Right into the twentieth century and until the fire and earthquake of 1906 put a period to its golden age and unreconstructed ways, San Francisco clung to the grand manner. It is notable that the most expensive convocation of musical talent in the entire world including Caruso, Eames, Sembrich, Plancon, Rossi, Hertz, Alten and Van Rooey was playing at the Opera House and that the first casualty of the quake at 5:13 in the morning was the magnificent crystal chandelier above the orchestra stalls, reported to be the finest and most costly in the entire world. The crash of its falling was perhaps the loudest concussion, figuratively speaking, in America until the stock market debacle of 1929, for it sounded the end of a way of life.

A durable item of American folklore concerns the Great Fire which was part of the record of most of yesterday's cities whether they were mine diggings in the Old West or great metropolises like Boston and Chicago. It embraces the structure which, as the hour of doom struck, was saved or its salvage attempted through the agency of something other than water. When the mining camp of Greenwater on the edge of Death Valley burned, C. B. Glasscock, editor of the *Greenwater Miner*, attempted vainly to stay the conflagration with bottled beer, there being no water of any color handy. When Mrs. O'Leary's cow burned down Chicago with a great burning, Policeman Bellinger saved his home amidst the universal destruction with a stock of apple cider which was fortunately at hand.

When Humphrey's Castle on Russian Hill was threatened by the advancing holocaust of 1906, there was no water available but its owner saved his property with champagne, spraying the smoking woodwork with bottles of Mumm's and Crug's Private Cuvee which spurted from quarts and magnums in helpful Niagaras.

This might well be the epitaph of San Francisco's golden yesterdays. It was a city that, in moments of trial, turned to champagne.

LUCIUS BEEBE
CHARLES CLEGG

Virginia City
1960

From its very beginnings, or at least its first associations with white men, San Francisco possessed overtones of wealth and magnificence. On June 17, 1597, Sir Francis Drake, himself a magnifico and the representative of the most splendid monarch in Christendom, found on the California coast a "conuenient and fit harborough" which he took in the name of Elizabeth Regina of England, calling it grandly Nova Albion, the haughtiest title available to English imagining. The entire discovery of San Francisco Bay, to whatever part of it Drake may actually first have directed his landing party, was freighted with grandeur. His ship was named the *Golden Hind;* his mission in the Pacific Ocean, already accomplished, had been the seizure of Spanish treasure. His holds were full of Spanish gold and silver and the entire overture to San Francisco's eventual emplacement was one of color and imperial splendor. Even on the Plate of Brass with which Sir Francis commemorated his advent to San Francisco Bay was engrossed the likeness of Majesty in the form of "her highness picture and armes, in a peece of six pence of currant English money under the plate." San Francisco's first oriflamme and insigne was coin of the realm. From the first it smelled beautifully of money and what money could achieve.

One of the romantic moments in the history of the Western World when San Francisco Bay was discovered by Sir Francis Drake was confirmed by the tangible evidence of the actual brass plate mentioned in his memorandum to his sovereign. It was found by picnickers on a hillside near Greenbrae in Marin County and now reposes in Bancroft Library of the University of California at Berkeley. Every device of chemistry, geography, metallurgy and internal evidence confirmed the plate as authentic, a souvenir of the times of England's greatness and of the first morning of the Western Continent.

John B. Montgomery

Copyright Applied For.
Edwin A. Sherman.

Great events and golden names were a prelude to San Francisco's emergence on the universal consciousness. One of the events significant in the attenuated and not too violent transition from a sleepy land of Spanish ranches to a boiling outpost of the United States was the raising of the American flag (opposite) and taking possession of Yerba Buena for the United States on July 9, 1846 by Commander John B. Montgomery U.S.N. of the Sloop of War *Portsmouth*. The Mission Dolores (below) is a reminder of the Spanish grant days of California's tranquil and pastoral beginnings. It was built in 1782 and was the center of the town's life and activity under Spanish rule when San Franciscans found the "Mission warm belt" in the center of the peninsula more agreeable than the breeze-swept sand dunes by the water. Originally the Mission was located on an inlet of the Bay known as the Laguna de los Dolores, but this, like New York's Collect Pond that was once a feature of lower Manhattan Island, has long since disappeared under building lots.

Fires and earthquakes were nothing new to San Francisco when the most epochal of catastrophes came along in 1906. They had been more or less constant since earliest times and the Phoenix rising from the ashes that is the city's heraldic device is witness to its long familiarity with combustion. A notable shake occurred in October 1865 and is recorded pictorially on this page from the yellowing files of two widely disparate journals of the day. Below, *Harper's Weekly* in its issue of November 18 depicts the effects of the quake at the corner of Battery and Sacramento Streets. Above, even more graphically, is the confusion verging on panic that reigned in a Portsmouth Square brothel of usually irreproachable *ton*. The view is from a subsequent issue of the *California Police Gazette* and the figure in the center of the dismay is that of a well known senator forced to flee in what the news account was pleased to call his "nether garments."

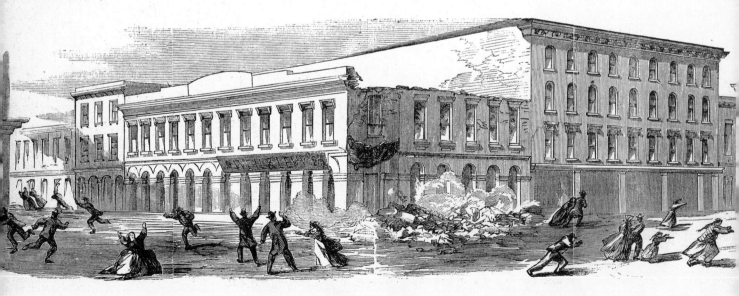

22

On May Day in 1851 San Francisco demonstrated its habit of combustion with the fifth major conflagration since it had become a city. Witness to the excitement inseparable from such municipal tumults was a young lady named Lillie Hitchcock, daughter of Dr. and Mrs. Charles McPhail Hitchcock, a West Point Army Surgeon, whose steamer docked while the ruins were still smouldering. It was a fated moment, for Lillie Hitchcock was to become celebrated in the annals of the entire West as San Francisco's leading lady fire buff and a celebrity of the first water and this was her first encounter with conflagration. Fire was to be the transcendent enthusiasm of her long and vigorous life.

JUMP HER BOYS! JUMP HER LIVELY!!

In the year 1849 when Argonauts were still arriving and the gold fever was at its highest, the biggest excitement in San Francisco's already frenetic existence was the arrival of the Pacific Mail Steamship Company's *Arizona* or one of the other Panama boats that maintained California's precarious communications with "The States." In the days before the erection of the signal station on Telegraph Hill with its marine semaphores, a large part of the population swarmed to the hillside in person, as is suggested by the contemporary drawing on the opposite page, when news of an approaching steamer spread through town. Below it is the Vallejo Street Wharf in 1863 when shipping was at a minimum as the war in the East closed many of the accustomed lanes of ocean commerce. On this page, the age of sail established continuity with the twentieth century when, forty years later, the *Kate Davenport* posed its classical figurehead over the Embarcadero.

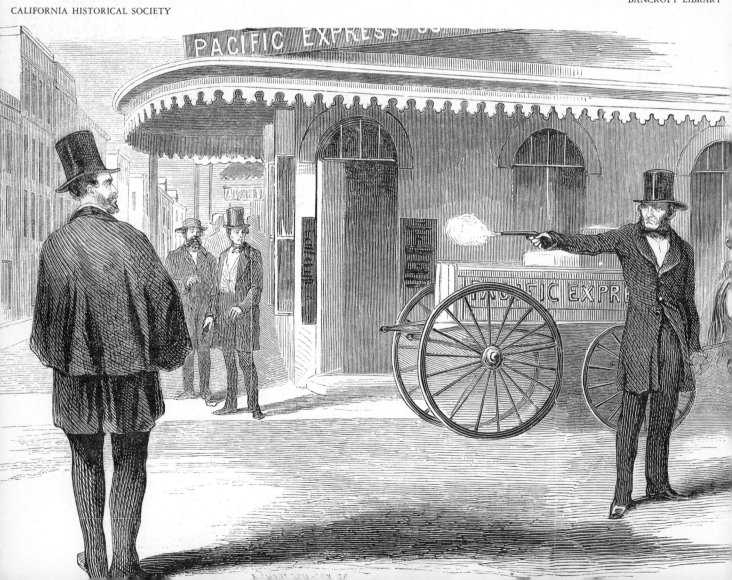

San Francisco's most stirring hours were those when the second Vigilance Committee became the accepted agency of justice and took over the conduct of the city's politics from one of the most corrupt municipal governments in the long history of American corruption. Sparking the uprising of outraged citizens was the murder of General W. H. Richardson, United States Marshal for Northern California by a notorious Italian gambler named Charles Cora. When Cora was denounced by James King in his newspaper the *Bulletin,* he in turn, as shown here, was assassinated by James P. Casey, a supporter of Cora's political fortunes. Summoned by the tocsin, the Vigilantes gathered and seized both Cora and Casey to insure their punishment and eventually hanged both of them. The Committee was composed of San Francisco's most reputable and substantial citizens and its administration of justice was the most salutary in the record of California crime. Depicted at the top of the opposite page is Fort Gunnybags, the informally fortified headquarters of the Vigilance Committee. On this page Cora and Casey are taken from the sheriff's office for trial and eventual execution.

An incident that lent fuel to the already blazing passions of Vigilante times was the stabbing of a member of the committee named Sterling Hopkins by supreme court justice and a Southern firebrand, Judge David S. Terry as the latter was being arrested for questioning. Terry was seized and his trial lasted for seven weeks, at the conclusion of which he was discharged with the recommendation that he resign his judicial office. This Terry refused to do until three years later and after his celebrated duel with Senator Broderick. Terry remained a troublesome figure throughout a long and eventful life which eventually came to a violent end when he was killed by a law officer in a railroad depot restaurant. When its work was done, the Vigilance Committee held a solemn muster and disbanded, leaving a notable record of disinterested justice and public service. So powerful was the example it set for law and order that when they were later organized in other parts of the West, Vigilantes in Montana and Nevada patterned their activities on its strict discipline and the swift retribution it administered where other law had failed.

GREAT EXCITEMENT IN SAN FRANCISCO, CALIFORNIA.

In far-off New York the affairs of California were very much news in 1856 and *Leslie's,* as shown here, devoted much space to the Vigilance Committee as reports of its activities came in via steamers from Panama.

ILLUSTRATED VARIETIES,

A Chronicle of Life in California.

"WHAT WOULD THE WORLD BE WITHOUT VARIETY? SOON HALF WOULD DIE OF SAMENESS OR SATIETY."

VOL. 7.   SAN FRANCISCO, SUNDAY, SEPT. 18, 1859.   NO. 20.

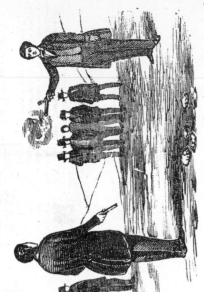

THE VARIETIES

J. Walter Walsh, - - Proprietor.

VARIETIES
Book and Job Printing Office.

Book and Job Printing of every description executed at this office at the LOWEST CASH PRICES.

Published every SATURDAY and SUNDAY MORN
ING, at 133 Clay street, Merchant's Exchange
Building, between Leidesdorff and Sansome.
Room No 11, second story.

TERMS OF SUBSCRIPTION:
Per Annum........$5 00 | For Six Months....$3 00

MAGUIRE'S OPERA HOUSE.
NEW SEASON!

PROPRIETOR............MR THOS. MAGUIRE
LESSEE AND MANAGER....MR. J SIMMONDS

SUNDAY EVENING, SEPT. 18th,

Will be performed the beautiful burlesque, entitled

CONRAD AND MEDORA!

Conrad................Miss Carry Nelson
Medora................Miss Sara Nelson
Birbanto..............Mr. Alfred Nelson

The performance will commence with a favorite Farce.

Dress Circle and Orchestra Seats............$1 00
Parquetta............50 cts | Upper Circle......25 cts
Private Boxes..........................$5 to $10

Box Book now open.   aug24

LYCEUM THEATRE.

Stage Manager and Director...Mr. ANDREW TORNING

SUNDAY, SEPT. 18th,

Will be presented the Grand Ballet Pantomine of

DON JUAN

Or, the Libertine Destroyed.

Sacramonch............Mr. Andrew Torning
Donna Anna............Miss Wallon

The performance will commence with the

DUMB GIRL OF GENOA.

PRICES OF ADMISSION:
Dress Circle and Orchestra Seats............50 cts.
Parquette........25 cts. Private Boxes........$5 00
Doors open at 7 o'clock. Performance commence
at 8 o'clock.   jy30

Scene of the murder of the late Hon. (no misnomer in his case) David C. Broderick, in San Mateo county.

THE OPERA HOUSE.—The magnificent
burlesque, Conrad and Medora, will be
presented this evening by the Nelson
family, and what with the stage adjuncts
that the ability of Mr. Dowling will intro-
duce, the transcendant talent of the
Misses Nelson, and the unapproachable
burlesque company now at this house, the
piece cannot fail to have a "run." Since
their first appearance, the Misses Nelson
have been growing in public favor nightly,
until our theatre-goers are ready to pro-
nounce them the ne plus ultra in their
line. The entertainment will commence
with a favorite farce, in which Mr. James
Simmonds will appear.

THE RAILROAD HOUSE can take as a mot
to, the language Shakespeare put into the
mouth of Macbeth—"The cry is—still
they come."

THE LYCEUM.—The pantomine of Don
Juan will be the attraction for to-night.
Byron said of this individual, in his cele-
brated poem of that name—

"You all have seen him in a pantomine,
Sent to the devil somewhat ere his time,"

Mr. Torning's Scaramouch is said to be
one of the happiest efforts in that character ever seen on our stage, and that he
even surpasses Gabriel Ravel in the palm-
iest days of that great pantominist. There
being a first class stock company at the
Lyceum, full houses is sure to be the
reward of the manager's enterprise. The
"Dumb Girl of Genoa" will be performed
this evening prior to the pantomine.

THE IDEATICAL," with General Isaacs
to marshal its army of occupation at "Fort
Bitters," still continues to flourish, and its
waves to nourish most of the dwellers
corner of Sacramento and Front streets.

In the newspaper world of 1859 woodcuts depicting topical events were too precious to be wasted, and the editor of *Illustrated Varieties* used his picture of the Terry-Broderick duel on his front page and again on the inside of the paper.

---

8   THE VARIETIES—A CHRONICLE OF LIFE IN CALIFORNIA.

"Q ON A CORNER."—Our valuable correspondent bearing this euphonious nom
de plume, has, at times, hit extremely hard,
some of our friends. To such as perhaps
didn't expect such warm marks of friend-
ship through our columns, we must say,
by way of explanation, Mr. "Q" does not
by any manner of means know all our
friends, nor does he consult us in regard
to what he writes. Nor this alone. Like
all brilliant writers, he kicks at the idea of
our destroying a fine peroration (according to his views,) by drawing our pen over
a pointed paragraph and rendering it—
mortuus est to all the world, save the wri-
ter and ourself. Often, too, business, matter and ourself. Often, too, business, mat-
spiritualism, renders it necessary for us
to hand to the printers our correspondent's
letters, and they appear in our columns
without supervision, and whilst at it, we
may confess, it frequently occurs they appear, like a sinner's spirit, before their
judges with all their sins on their head,
and errors apparent.

This, we regret to say, was the case a
few weeks ago, when two of our most valued friends were dealt with unjustly, to
the best of our belief. One of the parties
was Mr. Clayton, whom we esteem very
highly, and would not under any circum-
stances wound his feelings or touch his
refined sensibilities. If, at times, Mr.
Clayton indulges in some singular flights
of fancy "at the bar," it is natural—most
natural. Where can forensic eloquence
be perfected, save at the bar, as the "San-
ate," in this bustling age, offers few advantages. Demosthenes, the father of oratory, perfected his enunciation, and became qualified to harrangue the multitude
by declamation on the sea shore with the
Syrens, mermaids and mermen for an au-
ditory, and the rollings of the swelling tide
on the rocky shore, were the thunders of
applause with which nature greeted him.
Mr. Clayton having a horror of cold water—whether salt or fresh—save for abla-
tionary purposes, very properly eschews
that element, as an arena for the development of his, and like a cork-screw in active operation, fully as good a commentator or ex-
pounder of the laws, as Coke, Littleton,
or Blackstone. So much for Mr. Clayton, such we hope, he will accept this our

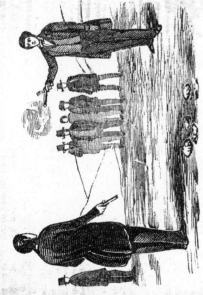

Scene of the murder of the late Hon. (no misnomer in his case) David C. Broderick, in San Mateo county.

apology, for the unintentional "dash" we
had at him through "Q on a Corner's" desire to give "all a turn." The other case
was that of a 4th street bookseller. With
this, "Q on a Corner" had nothing to do,
and as we can conscientiously say to the
world, as we did to the injured party, we
knew nothing of who it was intended to
injure until two weeks after its appearance. We do not intend to do any wrong,
we instruct our correspondents to deal in
facts, but, we having but one pair of hands,
and one pair of eyes, must trust much of
what we should do, to others, and thus
the errors. Gentlemen, do yo accept the
amende?

SACRAMENTO during the past week, presented a somewhat lively appearance, and
might pass for a thriving suburb of a
large city like this. The "fair," as a natural consequence, attracted many persons to the Capital, who were there, more
with a hope of being amused, than bene-
fitted thereby, financially, physically or
morally. The hotels and boarding houses
did a thriving business, and landlords
should get fat on the fat prices charged.
However, it was doubtless "all right"—it
being "fair" time, and no matter as to
prices, it was all fair in the way of business. Amusement seekers had places
enough to go to, as there were circuses,
several "side shows," too numerous to
mention. The "Opera," and the Bul-
chants seemed to monopolize most attention after the second night. On the whole,
Sacramento was a very agreeable place,
during the three days and a half we spent
there. Everybody seemed to be pleased
to meet everybody. Smiling salutations
and kindly greetings on all sides. It being holiday week, discord seemed to have
fled dismayed from the festive scene, and
anger seemed clothed in smiles.

THE OPERA HOUSE.—The magnificent
burlesque, Conrad and Medora, will be
presented this evening by the Nelson
family, and what with the stage adjuncts
that the ability of Mr. Dowling will intro-
duce, the transcendant talent of the
Misses Nelson, and the unapproachable
burlesque company now at this house, the
piece cannot fail to have a "run." Since
their first appearance, the Misses Nelson
have been growing in public favor nightly,
until our theatre-goers are ready to pro-
nounce them the ne plus ultra in their
line. My Precious Betsey, with Sim-
mond's "Bobtail," can be seen also.

Flowers flung their wealth upon the vacant air, and rich men often fling theirs
upon the vacant heir.

SOCIETY OF CALIFORNIA PIONEERS

A curtain-raiser to the tensions and dissension of the Civil War period was the celebrated duel in 1859 in which United States Senator David C. Broderick was killed by Judge David S. Terry near Lake Merced. The shooting was the result of a feud in which Broderick had represented the anti-slavery forces of California. The city was profoundly stirred by his death which some boldly asserted was an assassination as his pistol had prematurely been discharged. The Senator's body lay in state, as shown below, in the Union Hotel and 30,000 persons attended his funeral services in Portsmouth Square. Judge Terry himself was to meet a violent end, but not for some years in the future.

Times that tried men's souls elsewhere in the land came also to San Francisco during the dark days of the Civil War. Many of the early settlers were from the Old South and Southern sentiment was a ponderable factor as the Union was divided. Shown here and at the bottom of the page opposite are two Fourth of July celebrations in 1862 and 1861, respectively, the latter at the corner of Market and Post Street, which were in effect Union mass meetings. Above and opposite pro-Union sympathizers put to rout a group of militant Secessionists in front of the Express Building at Montgomery and California Streets in a faithful recreation of the time and place in the film "Wells Fargo."

In museums, bar rooms and the apartments of venerable hostels such as this memento of Victorian times at Volcano, the Mother Lode recreates more than a century after its golden era the flavor and atmosphere of the gold rush when all roads and the sea lanes of the world led to California.

There had long been rumors of gold in California, but the tranquil economy of the Spanish ranchers paid it small mind until in February 1848 the Treaty of Guadalupe Hidalgo made California American. Almost coincidentally with this epochal event and with a changed Yankee attitude toward tangible wealth, James Wilson Marshall (*page opposite right*) carpenter on the premises of Captain John A. Sutter (*left*) discovered flakes of gold in the millrace of Sutter's Mill shown below. Contrary to legend, the news spread slowly. Gold appeared in January; it wasn't until mid-May that Mormon Sam Brannan appeared in the streets of San Francisco with a dust-filled medicine bottle crying "Gold! Gold on the American River!" By the end of the year the news was officially confirmed in the East and the face of the world turned toward the Golden Gate. The rush was on that was to make San Francisco the cosmopolis of the Western World, a citadel of wealth and splendor in the minds of men, the realization of dreams of riches as old as the knowledge of the continent itself.

The veritable look of the Mother Lode is implicit in these two reproductions from daguerreotypes of 1864 in the possession of the Society of California Pioneers. The one at the top depicts a long tom rocker with an equally long bearded prospector activating it while his partner hauls gold bearing sand in buckets to be washed. The lower is the celebrated bluff at Michigan City which became known as Michigan Bluff, a comparatively deep diggings, as it looked in Civil War years. Above in the background is one of the network of wooden flumes which crisscrossed the Sierra foothills to bring water to the various camps of the Mother Lode.

THREE PHOTOS: SOCIETY OF CALIFORNIA PIONEERS

Rube Goldberg would have admired the complex primitive earth moving machines devised for removing the gold bearing sands from deposits bordering on the North Fork of the American River for processing at the rockers at Maine Bar in the mid-sixties.

The look of California's navigable rivers and inland waterways in the West's first morning of golden adventure is implicit in this contemporary painting of the stern wheeler *Governor Dana* on the Sacramento. Romance rode the vessel from its first beginnings in Maine in 1850 when it was built by a Yankee skipper with an eye to the profitable trade in the upper waters of the Penobscot. He secured a charter and ordered the *Governor Dana,* but upon delivery, Maine politics being as devious as the next, he found his run pre-empted by a rival. Undaunted, the owner had the *Dana* knocked down, stored in the hold of a sailing vessel and shipped around The Horn to San Francisco where bottoms of all sort were in great request and a fine, Maine-built river steamer need never lack a cargo. The *Governor Dana* entered the Sacramento run in competition with such famed contemporaries as *Antelope* and *Crysopolis* and for thirty-five years was a notable performer in the annals of the world's most opulent water haul. In 1853, shortly after its initiation on the gold run it engaged in one of the races that became classics of danger with the *R. K. Page* whose engineer, finding himself behind, doused his boilers with part of a cargo of coal oil with fatal results when they shortly exploded. The *Governor Dana* as shown here in a placid moment on the Sacramento was painted by Norton Bush, son of a pioneer San Francisco photographer, and is from the collection of the Society of California Pioneers.

All types rode the overnight steamers to Sacramento: the top hatted banker, the grizzled prospector from the Mother Lode, Chinamen returning to the diggings, the frock coated legislator, the crippled veteran, the broad hatted Mormon and the dude in derby and sideburns reading the 1877 equivalent of today's market letter.

So much treasure from the Mother Lode diggings rode the celebrated Sacramento River steamer *Antelope* on its down trips to San Francisco that it became known as "The Gold Boat." Here it is shown tied up to take aboard passengers and revenue freight at Donahue's Landing in 1882. Other steamers whose names were household words throughout California in the age of gold were *Yosemite, The Secretary, Senator, New World, Cleopatra* and *Ranger* and their logs were the annals of wealth that flowed in a seemingly endless torrent from Volcano, Columbia, Downieville and Angels Camp into the coffers and counting houses of Montgomery Street.

The deep mines of the Comstock Lode under Virginia City were a vast and complex operation and for four decades sustained a permanent population of 25,000, all of it engaged directly or indirectly in maintaining San Francisco as a cosmopolis of wealth and grandeur that was the envy of the Western World. In the Lode's primeval times, ore from the Virginia City diggings was freighted down the slope of Mt. Davidson to vast reducing mills along the Carson River in mighty wains driven by a race of supermen as shown in the Henry Poore's celebrated drawing "From Mine to Mill." In later years much of it was processed in mills at the head of the mineshaft, made possible by abundant water piped in a fabled syphon from the High Sierra, an entire mountain range distant. The photograph below shows Virginia City in 1877 at the height of its fortunes as the greatest mining community in the world and San Francisco's most solvent and essential suburb.

The Comstock

Just ten years after the discovery of gold in the foothills of the California Sierra, a new bonanza was uncovered whose wealth, pouring into the banks and counting houses of Montgomery Street replenished the now failing resources of the Mother Lode and financed San Francisco's more abundant way of life for nearly fifty additional years. The wealth of the Comstock Lode in the bowels of Mt. Davidson beneath Virginia City was to total well over half a billion dollars in silver and gold, and the Nevada mining town, two hundred and forty miles away and across two mountain ranges, was for almost half a century San Francisco's most essential and cherished suburb. The deep mines of the Comstock created an entire generation of millionaires that included Senator George Hearst, William Ralston, Darius Ogden Mills, Senator William Sharon, James G. Fair, Adolph Sutro, later Mayor of San Francisco, James Flood, Marcus Daly who went on to greater destinies in Montana, William S. O'Brien and Senators William Stewart and John Percival Jones. Financed and operated out of San Francisco, such Virginia City mines as Con-Virginia, Best & Belcher, Yellow Jacket, Hale & Norcross and Ophir became household names throughout the entire world. The riches uncovered in Con-Virginia and California's adjacent shafts made John W. Mackay a national headline as "Bonanza" Mackay who was for a time at least the millionaire peer of John Jacob Astor, William H. Vanderbilt and other Croesuses of the East. In addition to the vast fortunes made by the mine and mill owners and operators, huge sums were made and lost in speculation on Comstock shares in the San Francisco stock market. Many San Francisco business institutions had their birth in Virginia City: Roos Brothers, for many years a leading California clothier opened their first shop in C Street, Levis, the Western working trousers were first manufactured on the Comstock by Levi Strauss as copper riveted protection for the miners, the Palace Hotel, the Mills Building, Flood and Sharon Buildings, the Fairmont Hotel and other San Francisco landmarks too numerous to mention were built with Comstock money. When San Francisco was razed by fire in 1906 fortunes made on the Comstock played a major part in its rebuilding. Until the deep mines in Nevada began their final decline in the nineties, through Pullman sleepers nightly connected Virginia City and San Francisco via the Central Pacific and its Virginia & Truckee connection at Reno. In its years of teem Virginia City was a dateline in the news as familiar to millions as that of Paris, London or Boston. A swaggering metropolis in its own right, Virginia City was socially and economically a part of San Francisco's being; it footed the bills for the most glittering and endearing aspects of life in the city by the Golden Gate.

After the Great Fire of 1875 which burned the greatest mining town in the West as flat as a collapsed opera hat in a few hours, Virginia City arose in less flammable stone and brick and for a brief interlude was again a name to flutter pulses on the stock exchanges and bourses of the world. Its institutions, *The Territorial Enterprise*, the Washoe Club with its membership of senators and rich millionaires, its 100 gorgeous saloons and brothels to match, its outposts and satrapies of Wells Fargo & Company and the Bank of California, its tumults and discoveries and bankruptcies and the dynasties it enriched and enobled in San Francisco and London, in Rome and New York were the stuff of golden legend and romantic reality. The Frederick House, as shown in the photograph, was handy to the Virginia & Truckee Railroad depot and got the drummers. Visible further up the slope of Union Street, the International Hotel boasted the first elevators west of Chicago, the patronage of the nabobs and a world celebrity for the resources of its bar and cellars.

44

Well and unfavorably known to his associates as Slippery Jim, James G. Fair, Virginia City bonanza king and later United States Senator from Nevada in the era of silver senators, was an outstanding addition, in the words of Oscar Lewis, to "San Francisco's bumper crop of characters." Spiteful, quarrelsome and uncouth, he was the very reverse of genial and urbane John Mackay and he furnished the press of California with choice copy whenever a dull Monday edition loomed. Upon one occasion, Fair had planned a gala luncheon to be served on one of the lower levels of Con-Virginia in honor of a group of visiting dignitaries to the Comstock including frosty and decorous Darius Ogden Mills, powerful moneybags of the Bank of California. The Cornish Cousin Jacks in the mine, however, mistook the purpose of the rich hampers and choice viands, imagining them the gift of a grateful management as a reward for their services. When Fair and his guests arrived the cold collation of champagne and foie gras had disappeared and the miners were in a mood for revelry. The scene, as shown below, later became the subject for a spirited drawing in *The Police Gazette*.

When San Francisco's own rich disorders flagged, the town turned to the howling wilderness of Nevada for vicarious thrills. Late in the seventies, it was enchanted to learn that John Mackay and Jim Fair, two of its richest millionaires, had risked life and limb to ride precariously and at breakneck speed down a lumber flume from the top of the High Sierra to Carson Valley. Even *Harper's Weekly* in far-off New York gave the feat, as shown here, a two page spread.

When Virginia City's foremost courtesan Julia Bulette was the victim of a sensational murder mystery and her slayer eventually hanged with enormous fanfare, San Franciscans read of the execution of John Millain graphically illustrated with an artistic woodcut in the ubiquitous *California Police Gazette*.

More delightful even than a hanging were the Comstock's recurrent bar room Gettysburgs and these, too, the *Police Gazette* furnished forth in full dress for breakfast tables on Rincon Hill as well as Happy Valley.

A Lively Row at the National Brewery, in Virginia City, Nevada.

The mines of the Comstock never "gave out," and there are probably more riches still buried in the womb of Sun Mountain than were ever recovered in the successive Virginia City bonanzas. The increased cost of labor, the depth of the shafts themselves and the decline in value of precious metals gradually made operations unprofitable. The population of Virginia City drifted away on the news of strikes at Tonopah and the Amargosa. The silver kings had long since departed once the richest pickings were exhausted. The International Hotel burned down; the once lordly Virginia & Truckee Railroad, tired of running ghost trains to a ghost town, itself became a memory. San Francisco's most celebrated faubourg was becoming a property of the historian and the antiquary. In the scattered necropolis of its several cemeteries, the past and its once vital participants sleep in the shadow of Sun Mountain, returning to the elemental earth from which, long ago, they wrested its transient treasures and the glory of a moment.

MOSS

For more than a century *The Territorial Enterprise,* published first at Genoa, then in Carson City and after 1860 on the Comstock, was one of the atmospheric names of the Old West, a newspaper of violence and gunfire in whose columns Sam Clemens first signed a story with the byline Mark Twain and which made and destroyed senators and governors at its whim.

As the lights of Virginia City grew dim a gentle melancholy settled on the once populous mining town. Old Pancake Comstock himself, for whom the stupendous Lode was named, drank his way as far as Bozeman, Montana, where he took his own life and is buried to this day. Shadows gathered around the fine brick mansion *(at right)* which John Mackay built in the hope that his wife might spend a few weeks each year at the scene of their beginnings. Mrs. Mackay never returned to Nevada and Mackay never spent a night under its roof.

An event of social and civic magnitude that stirred San Francisco to the depth of its being was the arrival at The Palace in 1876 of Dom Pedro III, Emperor of Brazil and the first actually regnant royalty to visit the United States in its 100 republican years. An affable and admiring monarch, Dom Pedro came to California fresh from the Centennial Exposition at Philadelphia where he had bought himself a private railroad car and received the homage of foremost citizens as became a royal personage. He is shown here receiving further honors from a California delegation in his suite at The Palace. The Emperor immediately identified himself as a man of sound perceptions and an appreciation of the finer things when he declared that nothing in his travels made him more ashamed of public buildings in his own country as San Francisco's newly opened showplace at the corner of Market and New Montgomery.

Whenever, to this day, the baths, parks, libraries, real estate developments and other properties are mentioned that bear the name of Adolph Sutro, famed in his lifetime as San Francisco's most energetic mayor, they are memorials to this benevolent old gentleman shown taking his ease at the township of Sutro, Nevada. A one-time cigar maker who was among the first arrivals on the Comstock Lode, Sutro dug his celebrated tunnel to drain the deep mines under Virginia City and made his fortune in the nick of time before operations on the Lode went into their long decline. He returned to San Francisco to become its most favorably remembered mayor and one whose benefactions keep his name green in a later time.

The first private car, the ultimate symbol of financial success and social aloofness, in California, excepting those of the railroad rajahs of the Central Pacific was that of D. O. Mills, recreated here in its operational glory in the High Sierra headed for the Comstock Lode in Nevada, one of the most fruitful sources of Mills' multiple millions. Having amassed a formidable fortune from Western mines, banks and railroads, Mills departed for New York to found a dynasty still discernible to this day in the far-flung and influential Mills and Reid families. His son-in-law, Whitelaw Reid, with Mills' California money, bought Horace Greeley's tottering *New York Tribune* and eventually the post of American Ambassador to the Court of St. James's, an honor to which his Anglomania beckoned him, as a commentator uncharitably remarked, as fast as his hands and knees could carry him.

PULLMAN STANDARD

HOWARD FOGG

There was no democratic nonsense about Darius Ogden Mills, and folksiness had no part in the frosty old moneybags of the all-powerful Bank of California who had no hesitation about listing his occupation as *capitalist* in the San Francisco business directory. Side whiskers, frock coat, flowered vest and congress gaiters, he looked the part he played throughout a long, powerful and acquisitive life as a towering figure in financial circles, first on the Mother Lode, then in Montgomery Street and finally in New York.

Indicative of the nation-wide interest aroused by the death of Ralston is this sketch published a week later by *Harper's* depicting the North Beach scene of his death by drowning. The Neptune Bath House from which he regularly swam is in the foreground while a dotted line in the water indicated the course he followed that fatal afternoon as he swam to the far side of the steamer *Bullion,* the ironically named vessel whose crew recovered the banker's body. In the distance are the stacks and wharfs of the Selby Lead Smelting Works.

What the Lizzie Borden murders and the mystery of her missing axe were to be a few years later, a perennial topic of speculative conversation for New Englanders, the mysterious death of William Ralston, cashier of the Bank of California, was to San Francisco in the seventies. The last afternoon of his life, after the closing of the bank, Ralston arrived at his favorite bathing establishment, the Neptune baths at the foot of Larkin Street, but afoot instead of, as was his invariable practice, on horseback. He was sweating freely from his walk, and Richards, the bath manager commented that it might be imprudent to enter the water so warm. "Oh, that's all right," said the nabob, "Just give me a couple of towels and I'll rub myself down first." He then disrobed and gave his light colored trousers and dark blue street jacket to the attendant, remarking that there were valuables in the pocket, a thing he had never done before. He entered the water in good spirits and then swam slowly toward the small steamer *Bullion*, owned by the Selby Smelters and anchored a couple of hundred yards away. A few feet to seaward from the vessel, he was observed to sink beneath the surface, but whether intentionally or from a cramp observers were unable to say. A few minutes later his lifeless body drifted toward the *Bullion* and the engineer recovered it with a small boat. Artificial respiration was induced, but hastily summoned physicians pronounced him dead. A coroner's jury brought in a verdict of "accidental death," but was it? San Francisco has been divided in the matter ever since.

The intense excitement that accompanied speculation in Stock Brokers' Row in Montgomery Street in Comstock shares produced scenes such as this when holdings in pivotal stocks such as Con-Virginia, Best & Belcher and California were bid and sold in an atmosphere of almost clinical dementia.

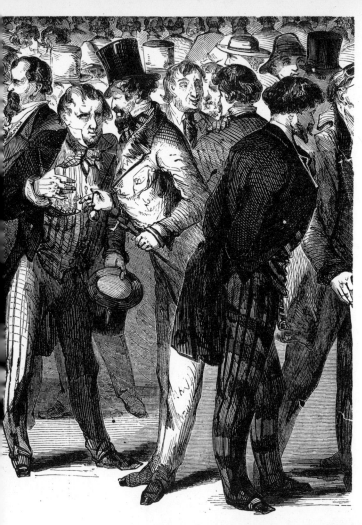

Inside news from the Virginia City diggings was the paramount topic of conversation amongst all classes of San Francisco society throughout the sixties and seventies. Confidential information from insiders or agents of the bank owners, whispered in clubs and bar rooms, especially the Auction Lunch, sent Comstock shares soaring or depressed them to nothing as might be most profitable to interested parties. Fortunes were made and others as swiftly disappeared. Below a Montgomery Street broker in Comstock shares who has himself been wiped out in an unforeseen financial coup dares his irate customers to do their worst. Suicides resulting from speculation were not infrequent, but no assassination is recorded.

The alternate soaring in bonanza and descent into abysmal borrasca of the mines in Virginia City more than 200 miles distant across the High Sierra was accompanied in San Francisco by scenes of sheer melodrama. Men of substance and social position, professional gamblers, widows with pensions, shop clerks, chambermaids, bartenders and every stratum of California society tried to get in on a good thing through speculation. Legitimate commercial ventures in California lagged because all capital was tied up on shares of Hale & Norcross and Kentuck. Below, in a rare old time photograph from the files of the Society of California Pioneers, a mob at the corner of Montgomery Street and California in the seventies surges in front of the block of offices occupied by brokers in mining stocks.

Word of mouth, the bedsheet size pages of the *Alta California* and *San Francisco Chronicle* and the newfangled stock ticker all contributed to the typhoons of rumor about Comstock properties which shook San Francisco on its financial and economic bedplates for two whole decades.

Whether as a result of the unwise enthusiasm of its cashier, the princely William Ralston, or as was darkly hinted afterward, a deliberate attack upon its credit by some of the Comstock bonanza kings, the Bank of California in 1875 closed its doors on a day ever afterward known as Black Friday. That afternoon Ralston went swimming in the bay and, again by mischance or by design, was drowned. These melancholy events cast a tremendous pall of gloom over the entire West and many of Ralston's most notable enterprises including the then building Palace Hotel passed into the hands of his associate William Sharon, the bank's manager in Virginia City. Although the affairs of San Francisco almost immediately recovered from the blow so that a few months later the entire community was once more rioting in bonanza, the closing of the Bank of California was temporary low water mark in the town's morale as is suggested by this contemporary drawing.

News of the tragic events of Black Friday was circulated by the newspapers throughout San Francisco and the suburbs with great enterprise, led by the de Young owned *San Francisco Chronicle* which mounted its newsboys on horseback to achieve outlying districts with the utmost in dispatch. The spectacle of newsboys on horseback, one of them managing an umbrella against the rain which lent Black Friday a touch of theatrical gloom, so delighted a staff artist for *Leslie's* that half a page in the next issue of that weekly was devoted to his drawing.

The Bank of California was organized as a joint stock company in 1865 when the first flood of the Nevada silver bonanzas was at high tide, with Darius O. Mills as president and William C. Ralston as cashier. For the next ten years it was not only an extraordinarily prosperous banking venture, but was popularly reputed to wield enormous power in Nevada and California politics, economics and society. Even the closing of its doors in 1875 and the death, supposedly by suicide, of Ralston failed to damage its great prestige on a permanent scale and it shortly reopened with assets in excess of $20,000,-000, an achievement only possible in a community of almost incurable optimism. By 1878 when the two sketches of the bank on this and the opposite page were made for *Leslie's Illustrated Newspaper*, the Bank of California was so firmly again the financial saddle of California that as much as $9,000,000 a day sometimes passed over its counters.

The eminently decorous banking rooms of the Bank of California *(page opposite)* were on one occasion at least the scene of plebian fisticuffs. In 1891 when he was past sixty, excitable, Irish John Mackay had a difference of opinion while in the private office of I. W. Hellman with W. C. Bonynge, an aristocratic Englishman who had given the silver king some minor personal offense. The two elderly millionaires slugged it out toe to toe until a dozen clerks, summoned by the alarmed Hellman, managed to separate them and get them off the premises by different entrances. By the time news of this stirring encounter reached the *Police Gazette* in far-off New York, Mackay had put to rout a formidable contingent of enemies. "He Landed One On the Proud Briton's Snoot", read the caption. "Bonanza Mackay Proves Boss Puncher and Routs Foes in Frontier Style." Irrepressible Ambrose Bierce in the *Examiner* commemorated the event in a mock-heroic ode.

The years of river navigation in California saw a frightful toll of life and property as a result of maritime accidents, the greater number of which were to steamers on the San Francisco-Sacramento run in gold rush times before the coming of either the railroad or any reliable form of boiler inspection. This graphic drawing from *Harper's Weekly* depicts the catastrophe which overtook the California Steam Navigation Company's *Yosemite* shortly after it had left Sacramento on October 12, 1865. The starboard boiler exploded with frightful violence blowing away the supports of the foredeck so that a ton of Mother Lode gold fell into the hold killing more than forty passengers. The *Chrysopolis* which was following her down river picked up the dead and returned to her pier, her bell tolling mournfully. "There had been four cocks of water in the boiler a few moments before the calamity," recorded the *Sacramento Union*, "but the boiler was of rather inferior English iron. The law now requires U.S. iron."

"When I awoke in the morning and looked from my window across the city of San Francisco . . . its fortresses and lighthouses; its wharfs and harbor, with their thousand-ton clipper ships, more in number than London or Liverpool sheltered that day, itself one of the capitals of the American Republic and the sole emporium of the new world, the awakened Pacific; . . . and capacious freighters and passenger carriers to all parts of the bay and its tributaries with their lines of smoke in the horizon—when I saw all these things and reflected on what I once was and saw here, and what now surrounded me, I could scarcely keep my hold on reality at all, or the genuineness of anything, and seemed to myself like one who had moved in 'worlds not realized'."

Richard Henry Dana in *Two Years Before the Mast*

What the sound of the cables running in the night in their slots was to the hills of San Francisco, the fog bells guiding the ferries to their slips were in the closing decades of the nineteenth century. Each bell had its characteristic and identifying tone, known to the pilot at his wheel who guided his craft by it through fog and night impervious to lights. After a time the hand struck bells gave way to electrical clappers, but the fog bells of the harbor evoked a mood of time and place in the hearts of San Franciscans in the far places of the world.

In 1900 the gold eagle on the stern of *Marion* surveyed the water of San Francisco harbor above its rudder chains.

In 1899 the *Province* of Liverpool jutted its bowsprit across the Embarcadero. Its figurehead depicted a modishly skirted and tightly jacketed woman clutching a bouquet of flowers to her bosom.

Three full generations of travellers arriving at Oakland from the East made the last spectacular stage of their journey by water across San Francisco Bay. They arrived, until 1958, at the Oakland Mole which was the western terminus of the Central Pacific Railroad and rode the cars to the dockside before boarding the ferry. For three quarters of a century, allowing for changes in the arrangement and architecture of the train sheds, Oakland transfer looked like this sketch made by a staff member of *Leslie's* in 1877 with the ferry *El Capitan* leaving its slip bound for the lower end of Market Street. At the San Francisco end of his brief sea trip, the voyager might experience such views as those depicted on the opposite page: pigs en route to market, rooting in the Embarcadero and a forest of tall masts of the world's shipping with Yerba Buena in the background. Before the bridges came, nobody could forget that San Francisco was a seaport.

Occasionally, in the thick fogs for which San Francisco is celebrated, disaster rode the ferry boats as it did in February 1879 when *El Capitan* and *Alameda* collided in mid-harbor with calamitous results. In a more tranquil moment on the page opposite, the much loved *San Rafael* plies the waters of the bay while, above, a steward on the *Oakland* enjoys a moment's quiet between trips back in the golden eighties.

The Sausalito waterfront in 1880 was characterized by the same jaunty Bohemianism it knows today. This picture was taken from the depot of the North Pacific Coast Railroad and the lagoon in the foreground is now filled in. The structure on the pier was the Arborvilla Restaurant run by the Kistenmacker family. In the foreground is today's Bridgeway, known at this pastoral remove in time as Water Street.

TWO PHOTOS: WILLIAM BRONSON COLLEC

In 1890 the corner of Market and Sacramento Streets looked like this and the brick building at the left was the Pacific Coast Steamship Company's office. The hand lettered sign indicates that pineapples were a dime while beards like that on the loafer in the foreground were a dime a dozen. "Union Bill" is unremembered by anyone.

72

A romantic assignment in the San Francisco Police force in the eighties was to the harbor patrol which played nocturnal games of cops and robbers along the waterfront with opium smugglers in the Chinatown trade, pier robbers and marine malefactors generally in a time of rowboats uncomplicated by the sophistication of steam or gasoline power.

Sail was still queen of the seven seas although steam and the expansion engine was pushing it sorely in 1885 when the photographer turned his ponderous view camera on *Sea Breeze* at anchor against a background of the San Francisco waterfront with Rincon Hill looming just beyond its stern.

Nor had sail lost its ancient romance sixteen years later when, in 1901 *Haddon Hall* of Liverpool docked at the Embarcadero where its figurehead representing King Arthur of knightly legend attracted the attention of the same photographer who depicted *Sea Breeze*. San Francisco was still, as it had been since the fifties, a port of sailing ships and sailing men although their star was in decline.

Standing before the walking beam that was the hall-mark of sidewheel steamers everywhere, the chief engineer of the old *Garden City,* Jeremiah Healy was a man of consequence in San Francisco's social hierarchy.

The smoke and glory that were the oriflamme of San Francisco's ferries are explicit in this rare action photograph of 1878 showing *El Capitan* coming into its slip at the Vallejo and Davis Street landing.

Nerve center and focal point of San Francisco's being in the years when The Bay was its principal artery of access and most of its traffic was water-borne, the Ferry House at the foot of Market Street was sketched for *Leslie's* in 1876 and photographed in 1884 to furnish the comparative views shown on the page opposite. In approximately the latter year the Marin-bound commuter takes the air on the forward deck of the ferry *San Rafael.* Identified in this rare old time candid photograph from the collection of Roy D. Graves, the commuter is (1) Edwin Griffiths, (2) E. H. Woods and (3) Charles Barrett. No. 4, lacking a first name, is Mr. Whittmore.

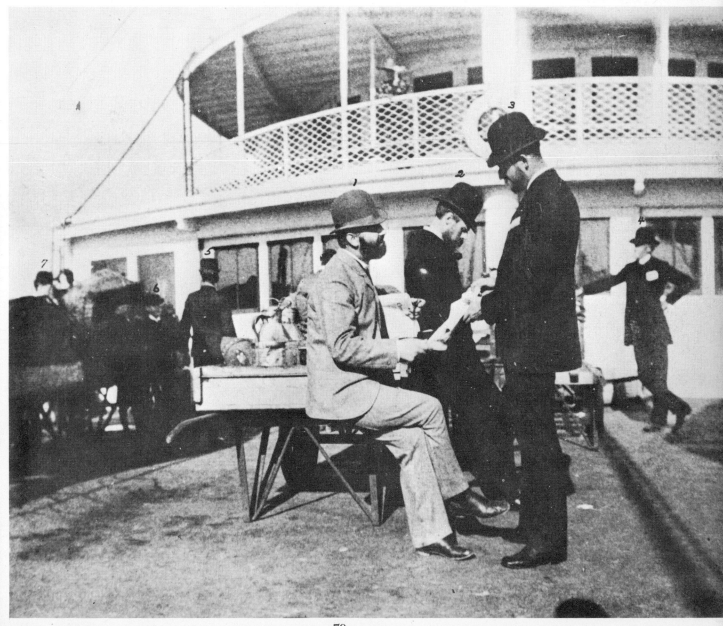

The hypnotic fascination of reciprocating machinery as embodied in the main crank shaft of the *Piedmont* evoked pleasure in a generation of commuters and travellers to and from the East who rode across the harbor on board the much loved *Oakland*.

In the year 1905 no pleasanter way to spend Sunday afternoon could be imagined than to take a sail, dressed in one's
Sabbath best on the open deck of the *General Frisbie* of
the Monticello Steamship Company as it passed on its occasions from the San Francisco waterfront to Vallejo and
Mare Island.

Three types of water-borne commerce are represented in this fine photograph taken in San Francisco harbor in 1885 as the *City of Peking*, representing trade with the Orient, heads seaward against a background of a sailing lugger whose province was the coastal waters of California and one of the Southern Pacific's Oakland-bound ferry boats with its connections with the steamcars and the rest of continental America.

One of the ever diminishing whaling fleet that once sailed from the seaports of New England, the *Charles W. Morgan* of New Bedford went into drydock in the eighties for reconditioning before setting its course again for the whaling grounds off the islands of far-off Japan.

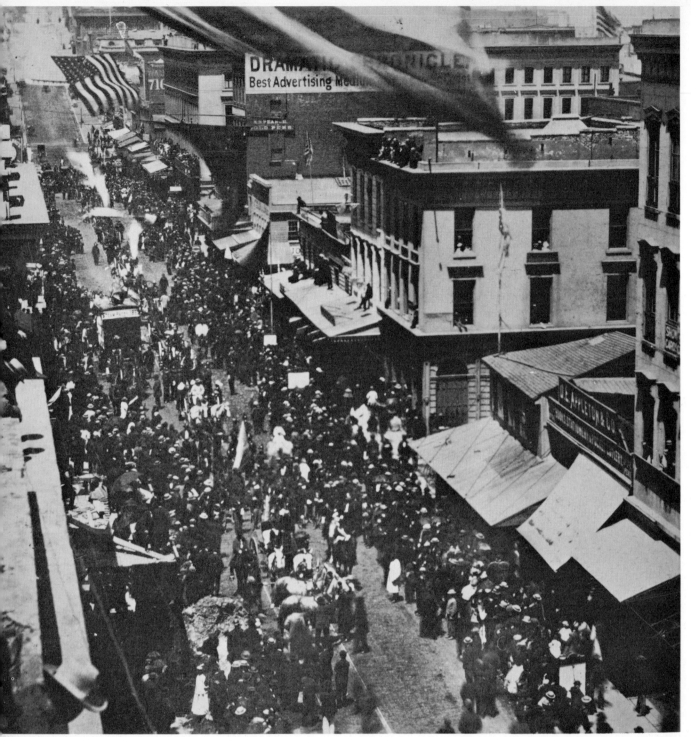

Nothing made San Franciscans of the golden era happier than an excuse to shut up shop and spend the day in patriotic endeavor in the nearest saloon. This they had in ample measure when the Gold Spike was driven at Promontory Point in distant Utah. The ceremony had originally been set for May 9, but the late arrival of the Union Pacific dignitaries from the East put it off until the following day. Nobody thought to wire back to San Francisco of the delay and the town started celebrating the event with the parade shown here on the appointed 9th. When the mistake was discovered everybody decided to keep right on celebrating and municipal carouse continued right into the eleventh for three full days of unabashed hurrah. In this fine photograph the parade has just turned off Washington Street into Montgomery against the background of the *Dramatic Chronicle* building, forerunner of today's *Chronicle*.

84

PROMONTORY

The most important date in California history that can be identified by day and hour, until the morning of April 18, 1906, was the afternoon of May 10, 1869 and the event it marked took place some 600 miles away on a wet and windy upland in Utah. Then and there, at Promontory Point near the northern end of Great Salt Lake the rails of the Union Pacific and Central Pacific Railroads were joined by a spike of California gold. It was the last act in the momentous drama of Manifest Destiny, joining the Pacific Coast in bonds of society and commerce and marking to all intents and purposes the passing of the Old West of pioneer times. The riding years of the Wells Fargo stages might be prolonged another decade in remote regions of Montana, Arizona and the Northwest, but Promontory was the symbol of a new way of life and new avenues of commercial exploitation. Below, drawn by the locomotive *Jupiter* is the special train which brought the private car of President Leland Stanford of the Central Pacific and other West Coast dignitaries to Promontory.

Overland travellers aboard the Silver Palace Hotel cars of the Central Pacific between Promontory and Oakland were seldom favorably impressed by what they saw of Nevada desert. The noble red man was usually represented by such Shoshone mendicants as those encountered on the platform at Carlin where, then as now, the railroad had an operational stop and passengers got down to stretch their legs and take the air.

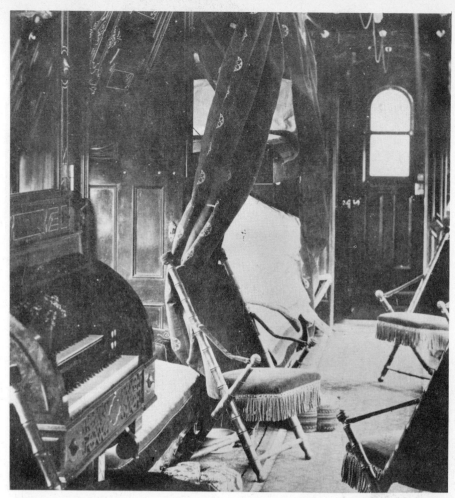

TWO PHOTOS: SOCIETY OF CALIFORNIA PIONEERS

In the early years of the Pacific Railroad, passengers changed at Promontory Point from the Pullman hotel and sleeping cars of the Union Pacific to the Silver Palace Cars of the Central (now Southern) Pacific shown in the rare old time views on this page. "I met with no silver whatever in the Silver Palace Sleeping Cars," wrote the Viscountess Avonmore of her travels in America. "The fittings, lamps, bolts, hinges, door handles, etc., are of the white metal called pinchbeck." Other patrons of the cars were more favorably impressed and everybody admitted they were a fantastic improvement over the trip around the Horn or via the Isthmus that had previously been necessary. Shown here are scenes with the berths made up, suggestive of snug comfort on the long night hauls across the desert, and the Weber patent organ to whose accompaniment hymns were sung on Sunday.

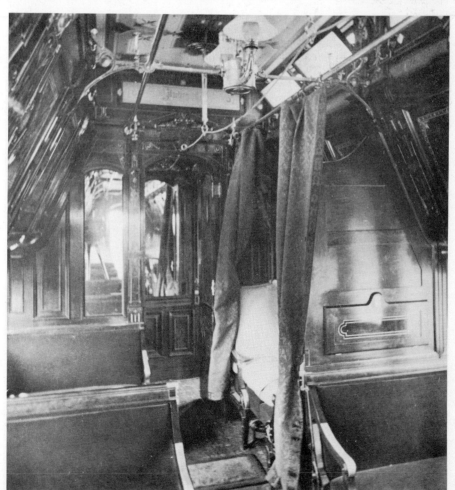

For many years the trains of the Central Pacific paused ten minutes at Cape Horn above the Canyon of the American River to allow passengers to view the scene where the gold excitements had had their inception.

Crossing the Nevada desert, passengers on the *Overland Express* received intimations of their approaching terminal as ranchers posted letters on the cars briefly paused at Elko and Battle Mountain. Then, at the summit of the Sierra crossing, they rumbled through miles of snowsheds, (*below*) mute testimony to the fury of the elements that had trapped the Donners not so many years before.

Fires and fire fighting have always been a major preoccupation of San Franciscans and when the officers of Tiger Hose No. 14 of the San Francisco Volunteer Fire Department posed for their photograph in 1864 they realized that the moment was a rendezvous with immortality. From left to right without reference to rank were James P. Ludlum, Matthew G. Searing and Neill Barr. No picture known to iconographists of the San Francisco scene is more explicit in the spirit of the occasion and its times. Below is a scene of flaming destruction from *Harper's Weekly* for March 1877 which bore the caption: "Great Conflagration in San Francisco—Its Wholesale District in Flames." At this date the Amoskeag steam pumper was in service in progressive American communities, capable as shown here of throwing a stream into fourth and fifth floor windows.

For more than a quarter of a century no civic jollification, including fires, in San Francisco was complete without the presence (*left*) of Chief Engineer of the Fire Department David Scannell. Dandy, wit and municipal character in an age of notable individualists, Chief Scannell was a toss-pot of homeric capacity and everybody's darling. Below is shown Broderick Engine in the sixties, named for the martyred senator, outside its house in Sacramento West of Kearny. On the page opposite is the engine and muster roll of Rincon Hose No. 6, founded in 1864 and one of the most social organizations in a fire department fairly awash with social *ton*.

One of the celebrated fire companies of Old San Francisco, Pacific
Engine No. 8 located in Jackson Street between Davis and Front,
boasted a marble facade with fluted Corinthian columns topped by
life-size statues in marble of firemen in full uniform. The picture was
taken in 1856.

Fire buffs, of which San Francisco boasted an uncommonly devoted fellowship captained by the immortal Lillie Hitchcock, gloried in the general alarm which was occasioned on April 30, 1886 when the Bancroft Building was gutted by a spectacular blaze and every type of apparatus on the city's fire fighting roster was called into action.

96

By 1882 the San Francisco Fire Department boasted the latest things in fire fighting apparatus, Amoskeag steam pumpers, high pressure water towers and hook and ladders with formidable extension and scaling ladders. Watching the hook and ladder take a sharp curve in answering an alarm was a never-ending thrill to watchers.

San Francisco's long record of municipal combustion has justified its heraldic emblem of a phoenix rising from the ashes, never more than in the two years between 1849 and 1851 when it was totally destroyed no less than six times by fires of known incendiary origin. They had been set by a gang of professional ruffians known as the Sydney Ducks who methodically pillaged shops and warehouses during the excitement and destruction of the successive conflagrations. Shown on this page is another notable blaze which levelled the entire lower city in 1853. Opposite is one of the fire companies of the period in front of its station and grouped around its hand pumper with a mascot mastiff and a notable convocation of well brushed tile hats.

99

The hanging in 1856 by members of the Vigilance Committee of Hetherton and Brace was covered by the press from a flight of steps in Davis Street. In 1859 the *Call (below)* was burned out of its plant at Clay and Montgomery but was soon in business again. Dull moments were few in the town's early newspaper days.

Destined to become one of the most influential newspapers in the Western legend of journalism, the *Alta California* came early to the scene and published its first issue on January 4, 1849 as a bedsheet sized weekly of immediately prosperous destinies. The next year it became a daily and its editor, Edward Gilbert was one of the first citizens of importance to suggest and later urge vigilante law on a crime-ridden city. The paper's finances and circulation boomed on a law and order policy but with the passing of time it came to assume a staid respectability and passed into the hands of James Fair, the bonanza king, who closed in its books in 1891. It had been one of the distinguished institutions of San Francisco's riotous youth.

Imitating their elders, San Francisco's newsboys in the nineteenth century were rugged individualists of the first order. At the right they scramble for papers from a delivery wagon in the seventies; below a group poses for its photograph in later years.

A property often fancied, along with Nob Hill mansions, private railroad cars and titled sons-in-law by San Francisco's nabobs, was a nice newspaper. Jim Fair owned the *Alta California* for a time. William Sharon bought *The Territorial Enterprise* in Virginia City to further his senatorial aspirations and later sold it to John Mackay whence it passed into the portfolio of Darius Ogden Mills. In 1880 the *Daily Evening Examiner* came into the hands of rough but ambitious George Hearst who also hankered for, and got, the toga. Senator Hearst's startling son, William Randolph Hearst, fresh out of Harvard, asked his father for the paper as a present and just as casually got it in 1887. It was the beginning of a publishing dynasty and empire of immense implications and has remained from that day to this the proud standard bearer of the Hearst newspaper domain. By 1890 the *Examiner* was a huge success and advertising itself as "Monarch of the Dailies" as it occupied the fine Examiner Building shown on Market at Third with The Palace as backdrop. It occupies the same premises today, rebuilt after The Fire, and together with *The Chronicle* is one of the two morning papers in a town where once there were a score.

Nerve center of a great and influential metropolitan daily, the city room of *The Chronicle* looked like this in 1890.

The Chronicle started business as a theatrical throwaway financed by the youthful brothers Charles and Michael De Young on a borrowed twenty dollar gold piece in 1865. A success from the start, it soon was a daily in the great tradition of the whisky drinking, gun toting editors of Western legend. The De Youngs feuded with everyone, gave better than they took and shot it out toe-to-toe with the opposition. This was its home in the eighties at the corner of Kearny and Bush.

One of the De Young's first sensational exclusives was the news of Lincoln's assassination which Charles overheard as a confidential message coming in over the Western Union wire for another paper. He memorized the long story, raced to his own office and had three extras on the street before the opposition appeared. Next day *The Chronicle* carried this woodcut, also a sensation of enterprise in a time when news illustrations were almost unknown. By 1873 the paper was doing a gross business of half a million annually and its first managing editor was Henry George, the economist.

Like many another frontier newspaper editor of the Old West, Charles De Young died of lead poisoning, his own revolver half out of his tailcoat pocket. M. H. De Young *(below)* lived long and made a considerable fortune, became a first citizen and public benefactor in the grand manner. The dynasty he founded achieved vast implications in formal San Francisco society and still controls the destinies of today's *Chronicle* as one of the most powerful of all Western newspapers.

105

The thirty years which had elapsed between the sixties, when the lower photograph depicting Gilbert's Melodeon was taken, and the mid-nineties when the board fence around the Bay District Race Track advertised Duke's Cameo Cigarettes saw the evolution of taste which had once decreed that a gentleman's only smoke was a cigar to that of a time that at least tolerated cigarets. In both cases, however, the older spelling of the various types of smoke obtained.

TWO PHOTOS: BANCROFT LIBRARY

Ask a San Franciscan of the eighties, when this photograph was taken, where was the heart of the city, he would without thought have replied Lotta's Fountain and the junction of Market and Geary, a votive offering from the volatile actress Lotta Crabtree to the city she loved. Here was a view that embraced the Fountain, the cable cars, the downtown urban life and movement so much admired and in the background The Palace, itself a sort of shrine of the city's most embracing destinies. It was a view that had everything.

Magnesium flares for night and interior photography were a new and perilous contrivance in 1893 when this evening view was taken by a forgotten cameraman of the Palace lobby with its quota of silk tiles and well tailored loungers, while shown below is the old newspaperman who sold the *Call, Chronicle* and *Examiner* on Market Street outside. A generation that admired rugged individualism took pleasure in this patriarchally bearded ancient who scorned hats and appeared resolutely bareheaded, a whiskered prophet of the early editions, in the most inclement weather.

Snow was alien to San Francisco both in Chamber of Commerce promotion and in recorded fact, but once or twice in the city's history it has been possible to throw snowballs on Telegraph Hill and the fur overcoats of pioneers were retrieved from seldom visited attics. Such was the case in December of 1882 when the old year was ushered out by a fall of snow from the Golden Gate to the High Sierra. Here is a view of Market Street looking westward from Stockton on the Sabbath afternoon of December 31. The four dark lines are slush churned by the hooves of horses drawing the four tracks of horsecars through the unaccustomed element. On the page opposite is the pictorial record of an equally unwonted occasion when in the winter of 1889-90 snow again visited San Francisco and the gripmen of cable cars faced unaccustomed exposure in a variety of protective garments. The inconvenience was of brief duration on The Bay, but in the Sierra the rails of the transcontinental Central Pacific were blockaded for two mortal weeks.

SOCIETY OF CALIFORNIA PIONEERS

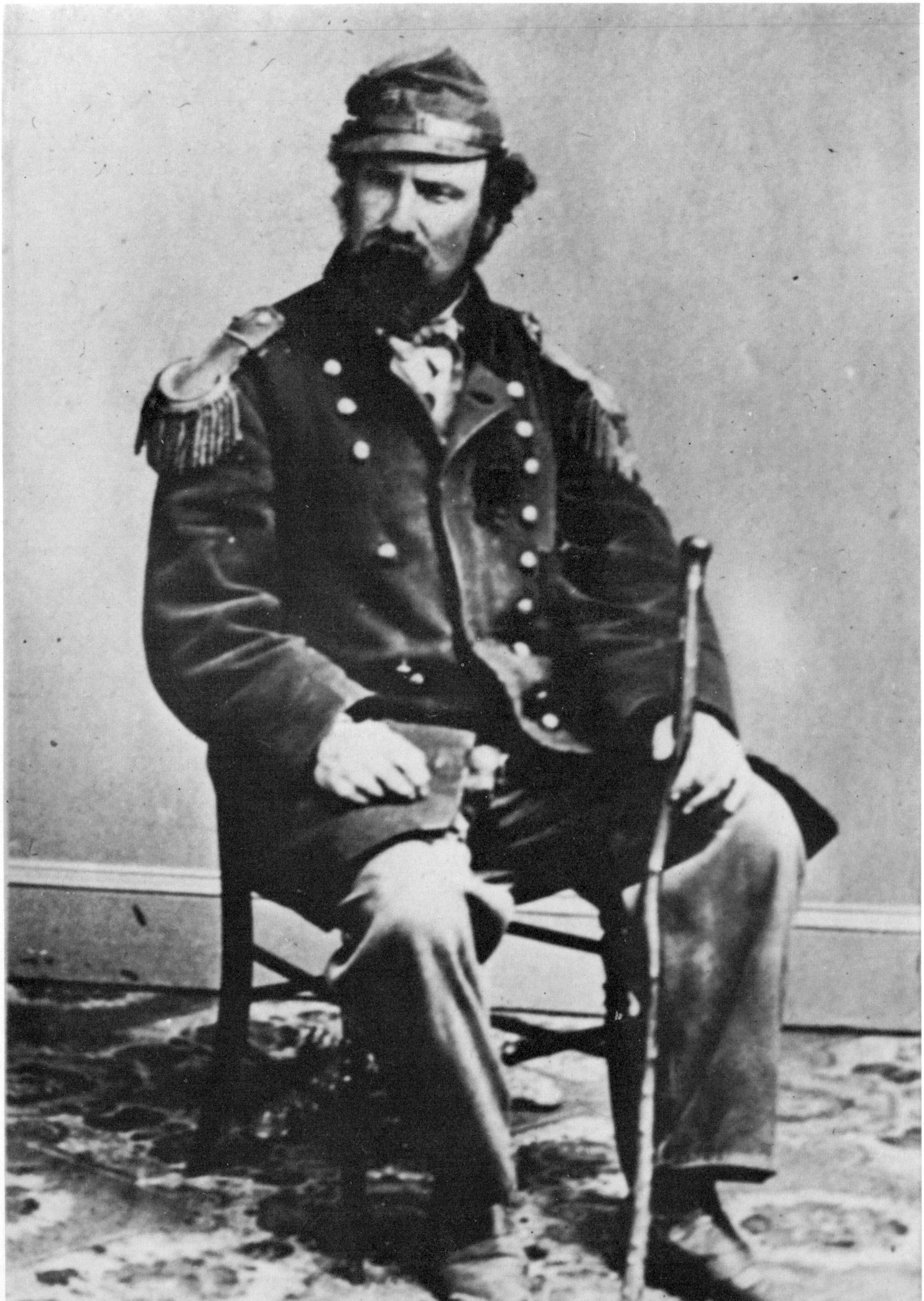

A stickler for protocol and etiquette, the Emperor Norton is shown in full imperial panoply: military tunic, dress sword, epaulets and top hat with a flowing cockade. The likeness on the page at left is an informal one, showing the Emperor in grumpy mood, possibly the result of a diplomatic slight, and with the military kepi and simple walking stick that characterized his more relaxed moments.

Most often repeated folk-tale of San Francisco's glory years is that of the Emperor Norton, the benevolent despot who ruled over the sentimental hearts of the townspeople for a quarter of a century. Joshua Norton had been a successful and eminently rational grain merchant until in 1854 he suffered financial reverses that gently clouded his mind so that he assumed the title and prerogatives of the Emperor Norton I of the United States and Protector of Mexico which he felt was in need of protection, too. He wore a vaguely military uniform and attended all functions of civic consequence where he was welcomed and his opinions sought on matters of public policy. Largely he lived off the free lunch counters of the best saloons and if necessity arose he issued imperial scrip which merchants were happy to honor in small amounts. On terms of perfect equality with other heads of state, he communicated with Queen Victoria and the Czar of Russia and issued frequent proclamations concerning the welfare of his subjects. San Francisco adored its emperor and when, in 1880 he died full of years and honors, it gave him a funeral many a regnant prince could envy.

A wonderful town to be a boy in was the sentiment of these three carefree youths of the eighties as they posed on their lawful occasions of delivering a growler of beer and selling *The Chronicle* in front of the old Mint on Fifth Street.

Beautifully groomed horses and a low wheeled wagon marked the arrival of steam beer from Wieland's Brewery, dispatched for the thirsty with strong men to manhandle kegs from the vats at Second Street between Howard and Folsom.

It seems improbable that hard headed old Peter Donahue would have approved this game of hearts played at their noon hour for lunch by office boys and apprentices in the shadow of the Donahue Monument at Battery and Market Streets, but nobody thought anything of it on a fine spring morning in 1904.

In 1904, too, train watching was a sport honored in the observance and these derby hatted youths have selected a vantage point near Ocean Avenue crossing to watch the Southern Pacific roll by in the smoke and glory that was railroading when all the world was young.

In 1865 Montgomery Street looking north from Market Street corner was already the financial capital of the Western World and the fresh flood of wealth that was to accompany the completion of the Pacific Railroad was still four years in the future.

In the same year that some now forgotten photographer exposed the plate shown on the page opposite these well mannered children were caught playing in Portsmouth Plaza with City Hall and the Hall of Records for a background.

The look of San Francisco in the sixties as few artists have preserved it for posterity is caught in this view of Howard Street by night painted by Arriola, a native of Mexico, and now in the private collection of Dr. C. Albert Shumate. Little is known of the artist save that in 1872 he was represented in an exhibit at the National Academy of Design and that in the same year he was lost in the wreck of a Panama-bound steamer. He is perhaps best known as the teacher of Toby Rosenthal. The view depicts Howard Street from Fourth to First Street in the mystery of a San Francisco fog with a number of notable structures lining the north side of the way and beyond the brightly lighted horsecar. On the near right is Union Hall, built in 1863 and used as a gathering place for many fairs, receptions and dinners until it was leased as a theater in 1885. A magnificent dinner was held there for the officers of the Imperial Russian fleet the year the hall was completed and in later years its premises resounded to the oratory of such notables as William C. Ralston, David D. Colton and Hall McAllister. Between Third and Second stood the Howard Street Methodist-Episcopal Church, one of the choicest pulpits in the community and in the same block the Church of the Advent raised its lacy tower. In the distance is the Selby Shot Tower where small shot for sporting guns was cast, a landmark in the sixties that was the equal of the Coit Tower of today. The lonely nocturnal street car was owned by the Omnibus Railroad Company, the first San Francisco public carrier. This rare painting was uncovered in mid-twentieth century by Warren Howell, the hereditary bookseller and collector of Western Americana of Post Street, and passed into the collection of Dr. Shumate from this distinguished source.

The solid, good substance of residential San Francisco in the sixties is suggested by this view of a Rincon Hill home looking northward over the growing and ever crescent city where a single five story structure as yet emerges above the level largely established by two story homes and business premises. Few would recognize the site of this sturdy, foursquare mansion as today's abutment for the sweeping Bay Bridge, but Rincon Hill was the first of San Francisco's fashionable residential districts and in its time was what Beacon Hill, Rittenhouse Square and Gramercy Park represented to older cities in the East.

Less aristocratic, yet quintessentially San Francisco is this homely view at Folsom and Essex Streets in the year 1885 where two white aproned housewives pause for the photographer while the useful and familiar horsecar passes in the background. This is the gaslit city that rises in the imagination of San Franciscans everywhere at mention of the years that were the golden noontide of its collective happiness.

Audience participation in the entertainment was a recognized tradition of the San Francisco theater dating from the days of the Mother Lode when chivalrous miners were so carried away by the stage action that they attempted to defend the heroine from the advances of the scoundrelly villain or loudly denounced the expression of sentiments they disapproved. When, in an early day play one of the actors was required to come upon a scene that so amazed him that he threw wide his arms and exclaimed: "What does this mean?" a wag in the balcony screamed "Side wheel steamer," a reference everyone understood to be the semaphore arms on Telegraph Hill. During a performance of Dion Boucicault's "The Octoroon" at Maguire's the auction scene in which the beautiful slave is placed on the block was so realistic that Henry Edgerton, one of the town's well known *viveurs*, shouted from his box "Damn the law! I bid $30,000!" The house applauded thunderously. When, however, a deranged spectator at a performance by Adelina Patti at the opera sought to throw a home-made infernal machine on the stage, San Francisco felt audience participation had gone far enough. It was gratified when the bomb exploded prematurely and killed its maker.

So immense were ladies' hats in the mid-nineties that the *Police Gazette* ran this satirical sketch of a male joker in a San Francisco theater who matched his escort's bonnet with a pyramid of male toppers. Later a municipal law forbade women from wearing hats while at the play. Below, outside the revered California Theater in Bush Street west of Kearny, is a group of matinee-goers made immortal in a photograph which caught to perfection the look of San Francisco streets in 1877.

The parlor houses of the Barbary Coast were the upper class resorts of San Francisco's golden age of prostitution. Most such establishments, according to Herbert Asbury, maintained from five to twenty young ladies in addition to the proprietor who was always addressed respectfully by the inmates as "Madam," and by the customers, for some obscure reason, as "Miss." Prices varied with the pretentions of each establishment, but many parlor house girls received take-home pay in excess of $200 a week, far more in today's money, while proprietors made substantial fortunes. Shown in these three groups are the madams and their girls of Barbary Coast love stores in the nineties, resorts of upper bourgeoise status, but not to be confused with such bedizened bagnios as that of Tessie Wall and other celebrated merchants catering to the carriage trade in more opulent parts of town.

In attitudes of studied abandon two Barbary Coast hustlers of the pre-Fire era pose for immortality with their pimps and the professor of the house retaining their services. That the date of this spirited scene is a fairly early one is established by the presence of the piano and the professor for, with the coming of the mechanical age, player pianos supplanted both and became a ponderable factor in the economy of commercial prostitution. The sale of liquor at advanced prices on the premises also contributed to the prosperity of the management and established procurers in an enviable financial status. While members of the staff, their pimps, runners and other technical assistants ranked fairly low in the San Francisco social scale, a successful madam sat well above the salt in the town's political and sporting circles. On the rare occasions upon which they were briefly booked for infractions of the law, they invariably and proudly stated their occupations to be that of madam.

FOUR PHOTOS: SOCIETY OF CALIFORNIA PIONEERS

Most powerful agency for Comstock affairs in San Francisco was the Auction Lunch Saloon (*right*) run by James C. Flood (*left, below*) and William L. O'Brien. Here, hearty and companionable bartenders Flood and O'Brien overheard tips which led them to make hugely profitable purchases in Comstock shares and later, as partners of John Mackay and James G. Fair, to spread rumors that might depress or stimulate the market as might be useful to the mine operators on the inside track. As members of the Bonanza Firm, Flood and O'Brien rose to affluence and respectability as directors of the Bank of Nevada while their families established formidable social dynasties still reigning on Nob Hill.

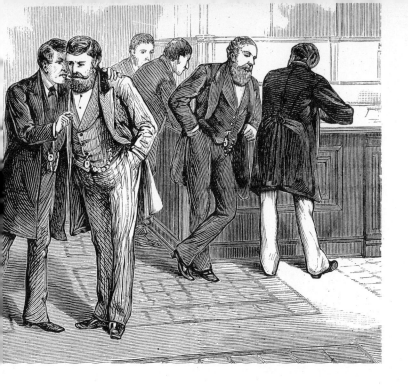

Confidences shared between the proprietors and favored customers of the Auction Lunch made and lost
immense fortunes in the speculative market in Comstock shares which, for three full decades, kept San
Francisco in a fever of excitement as new bonanzas
in far-off Virginia City continued to astound the
world. Even servant girls and elderly female pension-
ers known as "mud hens" played the market, staking
their savings on the chance of enormous potential but
improbable profits. Below is depicted the hysterical
enthusiasm of members of the San Francisco Mining
Exchange upon the news that "The Big Bonanza"
running to hundreds of millions in pure silver had
been uncovered by Fair and Mackay in the depths
of the Con-Virginia Mine.

Patriarchal Duncan Nicol is shown at the left behind the bar in his Bank Exchange saloon.

WELLS FARGO BANK — LOUIS MACOUILLARD

The anxious bonanza kings depicted at the top of this page have consulted their massive watches secured by Albert chains of Mother Lode gold and discovered that the sun has already passed the yardarm and that they are minutes late to the ritual of hoisting the first one of the day at Duncan Nicol's Bank Exchange. Hence their urgent progress down Montgomery Street toward the swinging doors of the town's most celebrated oasis throughout the seventies, eighties and nineties. Not only was Nicol the august and eminently respectable dean of San Francisco bartenders; he was celebrated throughout the world as the inventor and sole patentee of Pisco Punch, a secret arrangement of Peruvian brandy which inspired Rudyard Kipling to poetry and for an entire generation was the ranking drink of the nabobs. Two to a customer was as many as Nicol would serve. "It's as many as a proper gentleman can handle and I'll serve no others," he said and nobody took liberties with this rule. The almost unearthly sanctity of the Bank Exchange and the ambrosial quality of Duncan's Pisco have been enshrined as one of the great San Francisco legends, and the beautiful blue porcelain handles of his beer pumps are visible to this day at the Society of California Pioneers.

Steam beer was a brew and beverage indigenous to San Francisco and for many decades was specially manufactured by the California and Anchor Breweries and by their counterparts in Oakland where steam also enjoyed a vast regional vogue that long outlasted the nineties. As is suggested by this interior of the White Horse Saloon before the turn of the century, steam beer required special handling and storage. It was uncommonly light and frothy and its volatile qualities made a quantity of collar inevitable, hence the drip pans under the individual spigots. It was a new beer, fermented in great oak barrels, far stronger than conventional beer kegs, to resist the pressure it built up. Contrary to the suggestion implicit in its name, it was served chilled like all other beers, but its tendency to excessive foam made blowing the collar off a mug of steam an inevitable ritual which distinguished its drinkers from other customers at the bar. Steam beer long held an hold on the affections of Californians and only disappeared from general availability a few years ago.

Much of the community life of San Francisco's spacious years centered in its bar rooms such as that of Baldwin's Hotel, shown at the left, and in less sanctified premises such as that which witnessed the moving scene depicted below. In it the hard hearted victim of a female pickpocket's crime refuses to be moved by her tearful plea for clemency and motions the officer to take her away and show the evidence to the judge.

WELLS FARGO BANK

134

A harborfront institution by no means to be missed was Abe Warner's Cobweb Palace at Meigg's Wharf in an alley leading off Francisco Street. A combination saloon and museum, its name derived from Abe's belief that it was bad luck to discommode the spiders, and their trailing webs were undisturbed since the premises were built in the mid-fifties. Abe also kept parrots of legendary profanity and monkeys who had the run of the shop and there was a school of thought that felt the place was an unmitigated trap. On the page opposite old Abe, in a silk top hat, is shown posed in a neighborhood group. Below on this page is his front porch. At the left, a corner of Abe's bar is oddly suggestive of a later day Trader Vic's, a resort it antedated by nearly a century as a San Francisco landmark.

TWO PHOTOS: GRAHAME HARDY COLLECTION

In the eighties and nineties the Cliff House at the Seal Rocks was a favorite rendezvous for Sunday drivers of stylish horse rigs and later for primeval motorists and wildly attired bicycle riders. Between times it enjoyed a racy reputation as the scene of wild parties which, in the telling, bordered on the orgiastic. The two spirited drawings on these pages from the pink pages of *The Police Gazette*, while boldly ascribed to San Francisco's uninhibited night life, prudently refrained from identifying the exact scene of revelry, but many knowing citizens were sure the editors meant the Cliff House. The indisputable record that the Cliff House burned down three times and once exploded from a cache of dynamite mysteriously stored on the premises, did nothing to abate its enviably wicked fame. Clergymen claimed it was the hand of God; others ascribed the conflagrations to mischance with the Cherries Jubilee or cigarettes actually smoked by women.

136

Woodward's Gardens (*page opposite*), for quarter of a century the town's most popular and accommodating pleasure resort had their inception when, in Civil War days, Robert B. Woodward threw open his extensive gardens and art gallery at Fourteenth and Mission Streets for the benefit of the Sanitary Commission, predecessor of the Red Cross. Woodward, a substantial citizen who had made a fortune out of the What Cheer House where the first a la carte meals in San Francisco were served, was so flattered by the response to his gesture that he turned his grounds into a permanent pleasure resort with a menagerie, sea lion pond, black swans on the ornamental waters, conservatories and balloon ascensions. Many San Franciscans lamented the bad judgment of a municipal administration that later allowed Woodward's to be subdivided for building lots, but while they lasted its gracious resources of leisurely amusement made a lasting impression and reassured the world that the town had time for relaxation amidst its urgent concerns for money and commerce. Other "gardens" than Woodward's were favored resorts on Sundays, among them The Fountain beer garden depicted below by Walter Yaeger, one of the staff artists who accompanied the Frank Leslie expedition to depict the West in the seventies.

TWO PICTURES: WELLS FARGO BANK

140

Often reproduced, but still essential to the spirit of gold rush times is the festive bar room scene depicted on the page opposite with three prominent types of the period in graphic evidence: Spanish ranchers in their broad hats and Mexican spurs, Mother Lode prospectors who have struck it rich and are on the town for purposes of rejoicing and relaxation, and Chinamen, also from the diggings, in the conical headgear and pigtails which identified them until comparatively recent times. On this page is a contemporary sketch of "a ball for the elite of the community," perhaps one of the popular and fashionable festivities given at Apollo Hall and always known as "the Apollo Balls."

Although inconveniently located for ready access, there was always something doing at the Cliff House and Seal Rocks out by the Golden Gate. On the page opposite is how Fort Point looked in the late seventies with the Marin skyline across the water and below, a curious benevolent ceremony of 1870 when water from the Atlantic was mingled with the Pacific to symbolize, as the participants declared, fraternity between Boston and San Francisco. The symbolic brine was brought west by members of the Boston Chamber of Commerce aboard a special Pullman train that presaged generations of tourists yet to come. Below on this page is one of the successive conflagrations that destroyed several successive Cliff Houses overlooking the Seal Rocks. The Cliff Houses, until comparatively recent years, had been characterized by just enough shady repute to lend them enchantment as a rendezvous, first for coach drivers, later for bicyclists and finally for primeval motorists in the dawn years of gasoline. One after another the Cliff Houses burned with great municipal eclat and the present occupant of the site is the fourth of that historic name.

Sporting life in San Francisco was represented *(below)* by a group of turfmen at the Bay District race track in the eighties consulting *The Chronicle* for the list of starters. At the right a gay dog of the gay nineties urges a friend to have just one more before venturing out into the dangerous sunlight and fresh air.

A resort of less questionable moral tone than those depicted on the page opposite was Piedmont Springs, a favorite health resort of the Contra Costa. In this view taken in the seventies appears Samuel Langhorn Clemens, otherwise Mark Twain in an unfamiliar temperance pose. The original photograph was taken by Bradley & Rulofson, a firm which boasted "the only ELEVATOR connected with a Photographic Gallery in the world."

California politics in the seventies were notoriously and explicitly corrupt. Sacramento was a dull town and legislators came to San Francisco for fun and games. Senators, magistrates and other servants of the sovereign people were among the first to be invited to the openings of new pleasure resorts and in the above frame a contemporary artist has depicted how catastrophe overtook a Supreme Court judge when he tripped and fell, splitting the back of his dress coat at the inaugural of a stylish new brothel in O'Farrell Street. Below is a gaming parlors whose best patrons were members of the state legislature on the town.

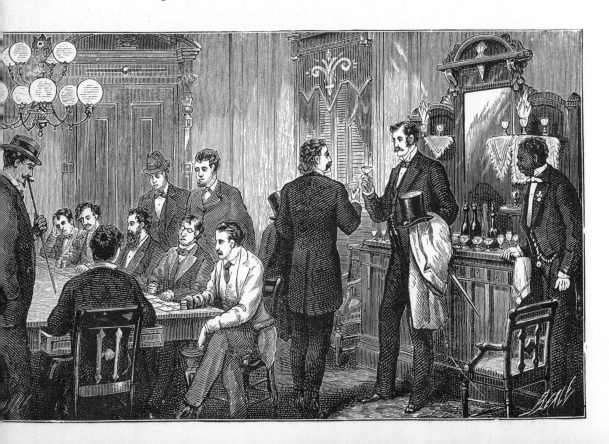

Although at various times the Bella Union in Portsmouth Square housed legitimate dramatic productions, its bright and evil celebrity in the sixties derived from its premises as a resort of gamblers, prostitutes and their fancy men, bunco steerers, professional harpies and honky tonk characters generally. The civil authorities were constantly called on to suppress disorders there and no visiting fireman was considered to have had the grand tour of the town until he had at least once visited its most notorious sin spot. On the side of The Plaza kitty corner to the Union was El Dorado, an out-and-out gambling saloon with no pretentions at all to respectability as a theater or anything else. Next door was the fruit stand of John Piper who was to go on to fame and three separate fortunes in Virginia City as one of the foremost theatrical impressarios of the Coast and owner of Piper's Opera.

NIGHT LIFE

Among the fragrant legends of old San Francisco, the Poodle Dog cafe at several addresses before the Fire achieved the status and dimension of a national institution, the peer of perfumed iniquity in upstairs dining rooms at Sherry's and the cottages of the United States Hotel at Saratoga. No small part of this celebrity derived from James K. Fox's *National Police Gazette* which attributed all high life by the Golden Gate such as the scene of licentious revelry below to the *cabinets particuliers* at the most famous of San Francisco night spots.

When the *National Police Gazette* in 1885 (not to be confused with the by now vanished *California Police Gazette*) wanted to alarm the patrons of a thousand barber shops and pool halls across the nation with the depraved morals of the time, it captioned this spirited scene: "Saved From a Flaming Fate By the Bubbly: How Quick Thinking and Mumm's Extra Dry Prevented Tragedy in the Poodle Dog Cafe in San Francisco."

One of the cultural advantages of life in the San Francisco sixties was weekly communion with *The California Police Gazette*, a sort of Golden Gate preview of *Confidential* which was regarded as devotional reading in the town's barber shops, pool halls and establishments of masculine relaxation generally. *The California Police Gazette* had no connection with its New York counterpart of similar name, although in the era of its flowering around Montgomery Street the *National Police Gazette* was making its first bid for fame and circulation in the East, publishing the names of draft dodgers and deserters from the Union armies. Rape, adultery, prostitution and carnal endeavor generally were the preoccupation of *The California Police Gazette* and its columns were spaced out with shootings, stabbings, bullfights, assaults and other tumults on a spirited and wholesale basis. It belonged, as a commentator remarked, strictly to the go-now-and-swiftly-by-the-window-it-is-my-husband school of journalism and it flourished amazingly in the robust atmosphere of gold rush times. In an age as yet innocent of half-tones, the *Gazette's* art department had on file fifteen or twenty durable woodcuts depicting scenes of basic emotion and its accompanying gunfire which it used in rotation with captions to identify them with the news of the week. On this page are depicted, from top to bottom, a scene "in one of our pretty waiter girl saloons," Miss Beatrice Guerdillo shooting her seducer on Jackson Street, and "Frank Lines and George Smith Cleaning Out Madam Reiter's Bagnio On Sacramento Street." While guests on Madam Reiter's premises, it appeared that the Messrs. Lines and Smith had suffered grievous loss of personal property including watches, fobs, shirt studs and currency and, in crosspatch mood, had returned and wrecked the joint. It was the sort of thing the customers of *The California Police Gazette* just couldn't get enough of.

The domestic virtues, in the pages of *The Gazette* came in .45 caliber. Here Henry S. Johnson, a man who brooked no nonsense, is shooting his wife's paramour, an event which took place in the stylish Rincon Hill district and was warmly applauded everywhere including the Happy Valley which flourished south of Market Street.

The editorial policy of *The Gazette* was firmly anti-Chinese and in this drawing white supremacy is being asserted with a derringer on the person of a target unidentified save as "A Mongolian Ravisher."

Despite the existence of such blue ribbon societies for the promotion of abstinence as the Dashaways (they were supposed to dash the proffered cup from their lips) temperance had a fairly hard row to hoe in San Francisco's golden years. The fame of the town's cocktail route, its legendary multiplicity of saloons and generous habits of hospitality far overshadowed the impact of various crusades for the abatement of strong waters. An outstanding advocate of the straight and narrow path was Dr. Henry D. Cogswell, a Forty-niner who was so revolted by the alcoholic excesses of the Argonauts that he conducted a one man crusade against whisky which took the form of erecting statues to himself, as shown on the opposite page, in communities which were agreeable to accepting them. Here Cogswell poses as a good example with a glass of municipal water at the corner of California and Drumm Street. Unhappily temptation lurked even in the shadow of salvation and the presence of a saloon is visible no more than a seltzer squirt away at the left of the picture. On this page a group of anti-Cogswell sympathizers pose for celluloid immortality in the days when a bit was the price of a shot almost anywhere except at the Palace and at Duncan Nicol's Bank Exchange.

Always a theater town of the first magnitude, San Francisco enjoyed the players who arrived in the heyday of the road both for themselves and as an occasion for social turn-outs in all the bewildering styles of the silver seventies. The tradition of theater had had its inception in the gold rush fifties when young Edwin Booth had toured the Mother Lode diggings with his father, the erratic old Junius Brutus Booth, and been continued by such seasoned troupers as Mrs. Judah, John McCullough and Lawrence Barrett, the last of whom in 1870 opened the much loved California Theater in a veritable explosion of gilt and plush and social fanfare. Barrett was to return again and again to the Pacific Coast as one of the most durable and admired of players and in the early eighties scored a resounding success in a now almost forgotten play, "Francesca de Rimini," a splendid farrago of medieval passion, adultery and murder in the grand manner of the time. Here Barrett is shown in the final scene of "Francesca" as drawn by Rufus Zogbaum for *Harper's*, the stage strewn with noble corpses of which he is presently to make himself one.

The San Francisco stage had its moments of exaltation and of low comedy on both sides of the footlights. Here in the mid-nineties a group of students break up a performance of Gilbert & Sullivan's then comparatively new opera "Patience" at the Tivoli Theater as an actor impersonating Oscar Wilde walks down Piccadilly with a symbolic sunflower "in his medieval hand." In far-off Boston in irreverent feuilleton, *The Police News,* a sort of road show of *The Police Gazette,* recorded the disturbance with the cut line: "University of California Students On a Lark: Hundreds of Them in The Tivoli Theater, San Francisco—They Own the House During a Performance of 'Patience'—A Street Telescope Man's Instrument Pointed at The Star Performers."

Wells

Fargo

& Co.

WELLS FARGO BANK

One of the great names in the lexicon of the Old West was that of Wells Fargo & Co., bankers to bonanza, princely expressmen and forwarders and for a brief but fragrant interlude proprietors of the Pony Express. Originally organized in New York in 1852 by Henry Wells and William G. Fargo, the firm opened for business as shown here in Sam Brannan's new fireproof block, Montgomery Street between California and Sacramento, on July 1 of the same prophetic year. Surviving the recurrent panics and descents in borrasca that characterized gold rush times in California, Wells Fargo in the space of a few years, witnessed the foundering of its every rival and emerged as the dominant banking and express company of the entire West. Like the names of the Pony Express it managed and Union Pacific whose cars it rode, Wells Fargo was destined to be one of the resounding romantic names of a time and place themselves the quintessence of romantic legend.

Within a few years of the scene depicted on the page opposite, Wells Fargo had agencies and branch offices in every mining town of proven importance in California and Nevada. Indeed the presence of Wells Fargo was the official certification of a mining camp and in many cases its arrival was the occasion for adding the word "City" to a previously modest community name. "Whatever nook or corner of the Coast may be explored by the enterprising tourist," wrote a reporter for *Leslie's*, "he is greeted by Wells Fargo's familiar insignia, assuring him of being still within the limits of civilization and in practical communication with the world at large. So famously did the affairs of the firm prosper that by the seventies it had moved into the handsome premises shown here, also in Sansome Street.

Guiding geniuses of Wells Fargo's destinies were its President Lloyd Tevis (*left*) and its great General Manager John Valentine. Like James Ben Ali Haggin, a native Kentuckian, Tevis lived to be one of the swaggering magnificoes of San Francisco's golden era and found a family dynasty which flourishes in California to this day.

WELLS FARGO BANK

Early in the years of Mother Lode gold, Wells Fargo laid a possessive hand on the express business in California, profiting by the mistakes of others and gaining advantage by its own aggressiveness and impeccable honor which guaranteed shippers against loss of property in its care, and time and again paid on the barrel head when shipwreck, robbery or other mischance befell its deliveries. Early, too, it established a reputation for tracking down and bringing to justice, usually by the simple expedient of shooting, malefactors who took liberties with its treasure chests. "Wells Fargo Never Forgets" was the epitaph it reared on the headstones of dead highwaymen. On the page opposite the firm's austere early offices are shown when they were lodged in the Parrott Building. Below is a scene from Paramount's film "Wells Fargo" admirably recreating the atmosphere of San Francisco in the fifties as Wells Fargo drivers brought the mail from the Missouri River in twenty-four days.

PARAMOUNT PICTURES

Wherever the venturesome traveller went in the California sixties, throughout the Mother Lode and in the foothills of the Sierra, there was a Wells Fargo agency (*below*) a reassurance in the wilderness and an outpost in the wilds. If he crossed the High Sierra, like J. Ross Browne who drew the night scene at the right, Wells Fargo awaited him in the Nevada Diggings, in Carson City, in Virginia and Gold Hill.

WELLS FARGO BANK

It is improbable that any single banking and commercial firm in modern times has dominated the affairs of a community and commanded the imagination of a vast region as did Wells Fargo in San Francisco and the Old West. Only the fur companies of the Rockies loom as its peers in the record. Its affairs were ordered by route agents wherever precious metals were mined and money was banked and its name bulked large in the lexicon of the Western continent. In San Francisco its satraps lived in princely estate, guiding the destinies of a far-flung empire on wheels. On this page is shown one of its most celebrated retainers, Hank Monk, ranking stage driver of the Nevada-California borderlands, a national celebrity whose "Keep your seat, Horace" addressed to Horace Greeley became a staple of American folklore.

Beau Brummels of the frontier were the stage drivers, none more so than Wells Fargo's James W. Miller whose dashing attire, rich display of jewelry and pet coach dog were typical of the love of ostentation that was a hallmark of the knights of the lash. No visitor to the Old West failed to comment on the ducal aloofness and splendid attire of such stage drivers as Hank Monk, Baldy Green and Jim Miller. Largely they favored cream colored hats of the flat brimmed style known as "Mormons," superfinely stitched driving gloves of softest leather to match, gray frock coats to abate dust-staining, tan colored paddock coats in inclement weather and a great deal of jewelry in the form of Albert watch chains and gold mounted whipstocks.

Most celebrated properties of Wells Fargo were its Concord stage coaches with their dangerous shotgun messengers, as shown below, and the company's treasure chests reproduced here in silver as a presentation award to Chips Hodgkins, a driver, for saving the company's property on a number of occasions of violence.

This presentation watch was given by Wells Fargo to Aaron Ross, one of its most durable messengers, for his resistance to a gang of train robbers who held up the Central Pacific limited aboard which he was messenger and attempted to dynamite the express car into submission. Wells Fargo never neglected an opportunity to remember a faithful servant with something at once tangible and honorific.

The contemporary artist who drew this version of the great Central Pacific express car robbery was misinformed in some of its details, but it served to convey an idea of violence. The gold snuff box shown above was presented by Wells Fargo employees to Henry Wells in 1864, a reverse twist to the more conventional order in which the company bestowed awards on the staff.

"The Chef at The Palace" is testimony alike to the fascination culinary subjects have always exercised on imaginative painters and the prestige of William Ralston's magnificent hostel whose *chef de cuisine* has, from earliest times and *ex officio*, been dean of San Francisco's corps of chefs. Although the subject, like the painter, remain unidentified, it is presumed by students of San Francisco legend to be a likeness of Jules Harder who had come from Delmonico's in New York and the Grand Union Hotel at Saratoga to open The Palace and who posed for immortality with one of the pieces montées so dear to the heart of his gastronomic generation, an aspic of langouste bound, presumably, for the table of a bonanza king.

By far the greatest sight to see in the San Francisco of the golden years was the Great Court of The Palace Hotel where stands its successor of today, The Sheraton Palace, at the corner of Market and New Montgomery. Here, in a glass domed rotunda sweeping upward for six amazing stories in the heart of the most splendid hotel in America, heroes were drawn in triumph, celebrities welcomed and the baggage of the great of the world set down as they arrived by Pacific steamer or overland on the steamcars. The fame of the Palace and its almost unearthly devisings of luxury and convenience, of the opulence of its cuisine and the august stature of its patrons spread throughout the world.

THE PALACE

Some idea of how The Palace dominated the San Francisco skyline and towered above the rest of the city is suggested in the photograph on the page opposite as it rose to completion in the summer of 1875, while an artist's concept of the entrance to the Great Court reflects the glory the hotel shed upon the social life of the community. On this page, posed in attitudes of patriarchal benevolence on the topmost gallery of the Great Court with Palace servants at their beck, Lloyd Tevis takes his ease with friends shortly after the opening of the hotel. One of the authentic magnificoes, Tevis was president of Wells Fargo & Co., a breeder of blooded horses, art collector and one of the town's most splendid hosts.

The massive grandeur and majestic dimensions of the original Palace Hotel which inspired awe in an entire generation of the great of the world are suggested in the misty outlines of this rare old-time photograph taken shortly after the structure's completion in 1876. For three decades merely to register at the Palace was a hallmark of social and financial standing. Conceived and begun by William Ralston, the hotel when it was opened in 1875 could have served the needs of a community many times the size of San Francisco, yet it was never regarded as a white elephant but rather a focus of civic pride and the embodiment of San Francisco's love of living well. Until it was destroyed in the fire of 1906 to contribute the perhaps most notable single component of "the damnedest finest ruins," the Palace was the abode of kings and presidents, millionaires and the great names of the stage, finance and society. On the opposite page is an artist's version of a dinner honoring Ralston's successor Senator William Sharon who brought the venture to completion, and its menu engrossed for each guest on plates of purest Comstock silver costing $40. each. The Senator is shown seated second from the right of the speaker smoking a magnificent cigar. He liked for everything to be of the best.

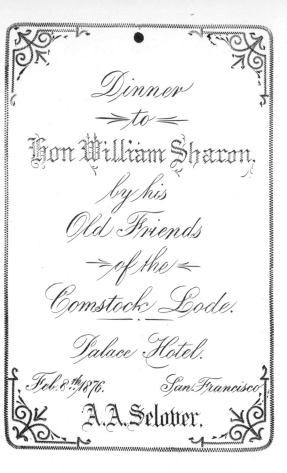

Dinner
to
Hon William Sharon,
by his
Old Friends
of the
Comstock Lode.

Palace Hotel.

Feb. 8th, 1876.   San Francisco.

A. A. Selover.

MENU.
Huîtres.
Chablis.
Consommé Royale.
Sherry Isabella.
Saumon glacé au four à la Chambord.
Sauterne.
Boudin blanc à la Richelieu.
Château la Tour.
Filet de Boeuf à la Providence.
Champagne
Pâté de Fois Gras.
Château Yquem.
Timbale de Volaille Américaine au Sénateur.
Clos Vougeot.
Côtelettes d'Agneau sauté au pointes d'Asperges
Sorbet.
Becassines au Cresson.
Château Margeaux.
Salade à la Française.
DESSERT.

One of the great attractions of the new and truly palatial Palace Hotel were the elevators, reportedly the first in a public premises west of Chicago and known at the time as "rising rooms." San Francisco's day of days in the seventies was the reception given President Ulysses S. Grant when he returned to California after a trip around the world and was drawn to his apartment in The Palace by a chariot with snow white horses as shown below. On the opposite page is a contemporary drawing from *Leslie's* showing Market Street looking east from O'Farrell with horse cars in motion and The Palace dominating the middle distance, as it did indeed the entire town.

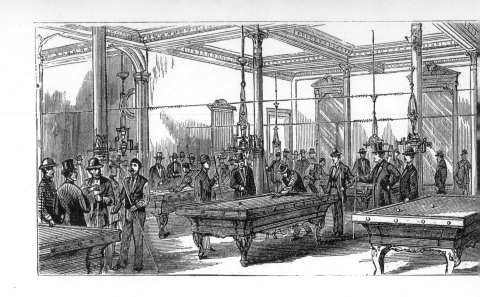

Lucky Baldwin

As typical of the San Francisco seventies it glorified as its rival, The Palace down the street, was the splendid hotel built at Powell and Market by Elias J. Baldwin, known in his lifetime and to posterity as "Lucky" and a man who gathered scandal as he gathered millions. Baldwin eyed The Palace, begun by Ralston and completed by Senator Sharon, with envy and announced that he was going to build the finest hotel west of New York City, bar none, if it took his enormous Comstock fortune to do it. The Baldwin Hotel very nearly accomplished both these aims and was a very fine thing indeed to which San Franciscans for an entire generation pointed with unabashed pride, although the character of its owner prevented it from enjoying the cachet of social approval which The Palace claimed from the beginning. The Baldwin had one thing that The Palace had not, a magnificent theater that came in time to have professional associations and social implications not enjoyed by the hotel. Baldwin himself, lecherous, cigar smoking, card playing and blasphemous, was typical of the frontier that made him rich. He made and lost fortunes, but he never lost a superb and spacious vitality and an equally superb courage. "By gad, I'm not licked yet" was the war cry of the old lion when encircled by his enemies, and he uttered it for the last time on his deathbed. His hotel, until its destruction in a disastrous fire before the turn of the century, was a pavilion of plush and ormolu ostentation. There was a $25,000 clock from Tiffany's that, as Mark Twain described it, told "not only the hours, minutes and seconds but the turn of the tides, the phases of the moon, the price of eggs and who's got your umbrella." The hotel vault by Herring Brothers was the envy of bankers; carpets at $30. a yard were ordered from Europe quite literally by the mile. There were pianos, then a hallmark of expensive gentility, everywhere and the Baldwin bar enjoyed a fame of continental dimensions as the peer of the Windsor in New York and the Southern Hotel in St. Louis. In Baldwin's personal suite of rooms poker was played for formidable stakes and the destinies of Baldwin's matchless racing stable were shaped over oceans of Kentucky Bourbon. Just outside its door Baldwin was shot and seriously wounded by a woman who claimed he had "ruined her body and soul." Baldwin never bothered to deny the charge and she shortly showed up as one of the foremost madams in Denver where her armed skirmish with the aging millionaire was an asset and advertisement. On the page opposite a sketch artist for *Frank Leslie's Illustrated Newspaper* depicts Baldwin's Hotel & Theater in 1878 when they were among the fine things in San Francisco by no means to be missed.

The nineties approval of massive eating in massive settings mirrored at once the opulence of the community and the upholstered estate of the patrons. The restaurant at Baldwin's faithfully reflected the tastes of the period in public gastronomy. Sometimes, to be sure, creditors complained that the contents of the wine cellars hadn't been paid for and threatened to arrive with vans to take away the rare Moselles and lordly vintages of Burgundy, but somehow Baldwin was always able to ease a tight credit situation. In any event, there was never a shortage of the best of everything to sluice and gentle the patrons of one of the town's finest dining rooms before going to the play in Baldwin's handy theater, widely acknowledged to be the handsomest of all.

In an age when masculine individuality expressed itself in a vigorous profusion of beards and moustaches, the barber shop at Baldwin's Hotel was the peer of Duncan Nicol's Bank Exchange and the front office of Wells Fargo & Co., as a gathering place of the town's boulevardiers and *viveurs*. Here Joaquin Miller, the Singer of the Sierra, James Ben Ali Haggin and the incomparable Fire Chief David Scannell foregathered for trim and singe with a dash of Florida Water and to sneak a covert glance through James K. Fox's *Police Gazette* nestled prudently in the reading rack among more acceptable feuilletons, the *Overland*, *Argonaut* and *Chronicle*.

A sort of sneak preview of a far greater holocaust still almost a decade
in the unforeseeable future took place in 1898 when Lucky Baldwin's
fine hotel together with much admired Baldwin Theater burned with
some loss of life. Typically, Baldwin carried no insurance on the costly
structure, and its loss was a staggering blow from which his finances
never recovered. On this page a skilled cameraman of the time caught
on a single plate the close relations between San Francisco's fire and
police departments and the hard hatted politicians of the age. A title
for the picture might have been: "The Fire Was Incidental."

A wide gulf both in time and manners separated San Francisco's first hotels, some of which were fashioned from remodeled sailing vessels beached at the waterfront after their crews had deserted for the gold field as shown below, and the elegant public apartments of such world famous hotels as those of Baldwin's at the right.

182

Until the coming of The Palace to skim the cream off the carriage trade, the town's foremost hotel of quality was the Lick House in Montgomery Street whose most celebrated patron for many years was John Mackay, the Comstock bonanza king. A contemporary watched the arch-millionaire "step out of the Lick House in light trousers and brown velvet sack-coat, a broad felt hat above his keen eyes, to be followed by many admiring glances." That the glances contained envy, too, is probable for Mackay was so well off that at his death an associate remarked that he probably didn't know his own worth to within ten million dollars. The Lick was evidence of the success of James Lick, a Pennsylvania piano maker who struck it rich in California real estate and whose benefactions included the great Lick Observatory that bears his name to this day. World travellers reported that the antelope steak in the Lick's magnificent restaurant, as shown here, was one of the gastronomic glories of an era of spacious dining.

PAUL FRENZENY

Originally published in *Harper's Weekly* for June 9, 1877, this engraving by the distinguished pictorial artist of the era, Paul Frenzeny is a classic representation of upper class society in San Francisco's legendary Chinatown in the years before fires and earthquakes and the mutations of time destroyed its cachet of Oriental mystery and elegance. It depicts a feast given by a rich merchant, who stands in the center of the apartment with a long-stemmed pipe, for friends shown enjoying themselves with music and an assortment of viands dear to the Oriental heart. Even the facetious caption stating that "We have it on the authority of Mr. Wong Ching Foo that nothing in the shape of a dog, cat or rat is on the bill of fare" cannot rob of its congenial dignity a scene that in another thirty years was to become no more than a San Francisco memory.

Two aspects of San Francisco in the golden noontide of its fortunes most fascinated visitors: the wealth and wealthy ways of its nabobs and Chinatown, a city in itself animated and darkened by mysteries of the cryptic Orient. No one was more delighted with the Chinese than the celebrated sketch artist Paul Frenzeny who repeatedly drew them for the august pages of *Harper's Weekly*, which modestly called itself "The Journal of Civilization." On the opposite page is a Chinese holiday with all its conventional trappings and explosives; on this page Frenzeny indulges the inevitable preoccupation of all visitors with opium dens. Despite their reputation for evil, nothing could be less sinister than these establishments in fact where quiet men quietly minded their own affairs and indulged a vice whose dominant characteristic was utter tranquillity.

The wonderful photograph reproduced above from a negative by San Francisco's now legendary Arnold Genthe might be taken as the spirit and essence of old Chinatown in the years before The Fire. It depicts a wealthy mandarin in the traditional Chinese attire of a private citizen closely followed on his occasions of business or pleasure by his personal *boo how doy* or bodyguard, one member of whom carries his hand suggestively in pocket while others, also heavily armed, prowl within call. The great tong wars that shattered the peace of Chinatown at recurrent intervals before the turn of the century were conducted with the greatest ferocity and skill by the *boo how doy* of the various embattled chieftains and were largely unregulated by the police since they were conducted on a strictly intra-mural basis. When finally feuding between the Sum Yop and the Sue Yops approached proportions of all-out war the Emperor of China, Kwang Hsu intervened to restore what passed for peace. On the page opposite is one of the alleys where warfare once raged and below the well fed Chinese staff of domestics in a Nob Hill mansion of the nineties.

The street depicted at the right
was Washington at Brennan Place
in 1880. Below, at the same time,
was Clay and Dupont.

Although the peaceful vistas of a pre-Fire Chinatown shown on these two pages suggest nothing so much as commercial prosperity and civic accord, San Francisco in fact gloried in the wicked celebrity of its Chinese quarter as a scene of merciless tong wars, murder on an epic scale, the barter of beautiful slave girls and the romantic trade in opium. Prostitution and narcotics were institutional among the Orientals and the San Francisco authorities were disinclined, except on severe provocation, to interfere in the private affairs of the Chinese population. The first tongs were organized in gold rush times in the Mother Lode as mutual protective associations and soon achieved great power as thousands of Chinese were imported to work on the construction of the Pacific Railroad. Large standing armies of *boo how doy* or professional warriors were maintained by each tong and exercised absolute control over gambling dens, houses of prostitution and opium parlors. Their favorite weapon was a common carpenter's hatchet with which they clove the skulls of their enemies with great precision and it was from this practice that the word hatchetman passed into the American lexicon.

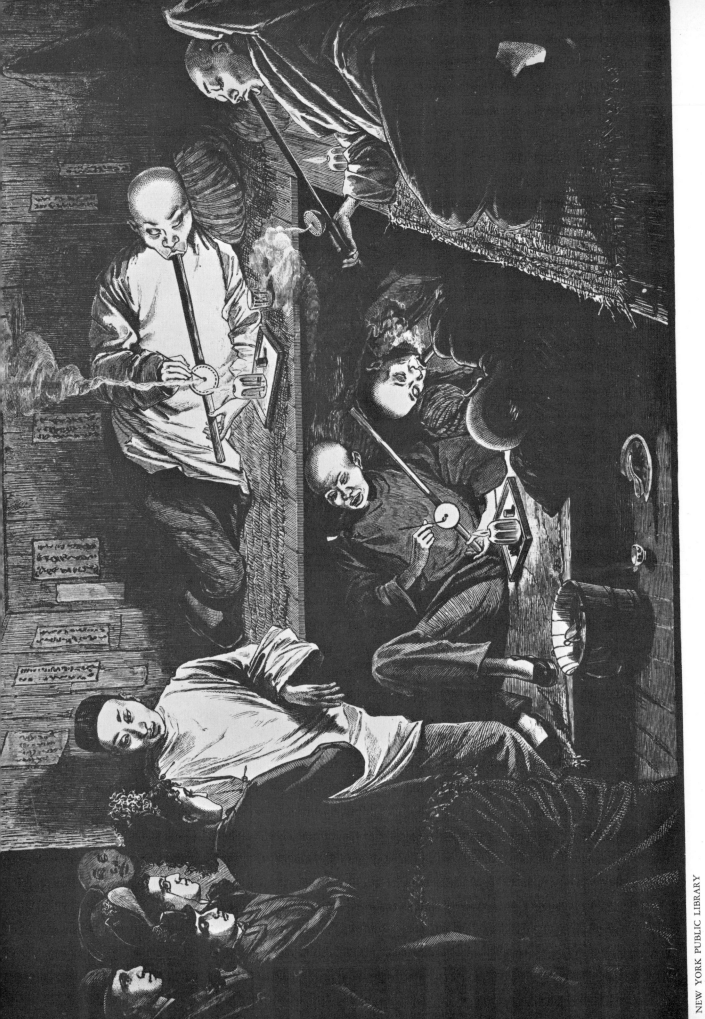

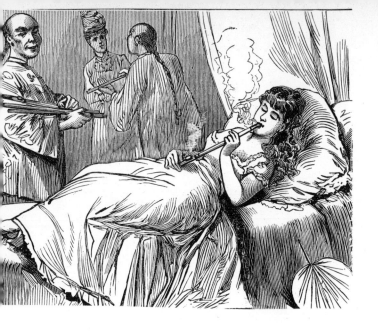

No theme of San Francisco so stirred the imagination of visitors and curiosity seekers as the opium dens of Chinatown and no visitor from the East had seen the elephant until his host had taken him on a guided tour of at least one of these comfortable sin dens. The sketch on the page opposite was done by artists Walter Yaeger and Harry Ogden for *Leslie's* in the seventies and the below photograph confirms its essential details. That "society women" occasionally sought solace in the poppy is suggested by the sketch at the left, a suggestion which chilled the spine of a generation that enshrined all its virtues in glorious and undefiled American womanhood.

The iconography of San Francisco's opium dens is of almost limitless dimensions since no artist of consequence assigned to depict the city's institutions could any more neglect them than he might the cable cars or ferries. It is an interesting commentary on artistic license that most pictorial reporters cleaned up their sin dens to a degree not suggested in photographs which show them to have been somewhat less esthetically attractive.

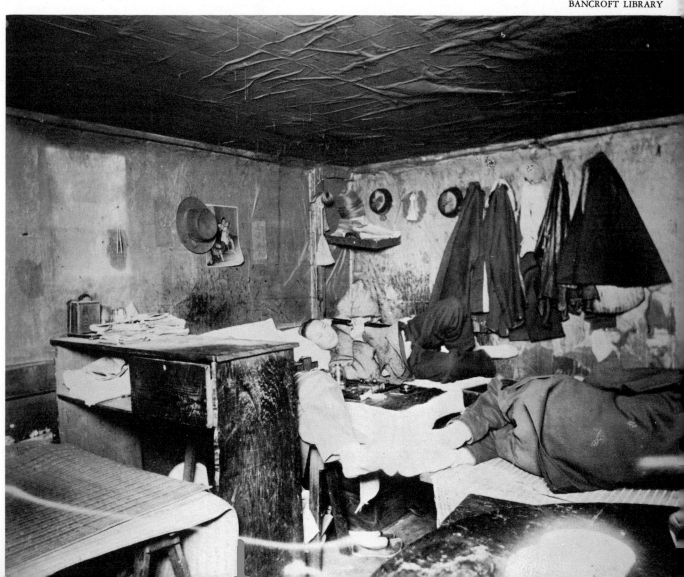

194

Street scenes such as this never ceased to engage the
professional attention of the greatest of San Francisco's nineteenth century photographers, Arnold
Genthe who took this interlude of teeming animation
in one of Chinatown's myriad alleys. On the page
opposite, some occasion of ceremony brings occiden-
tal visitors to the balconies of Chinatown as is suggested by the presence there of that hallmark and
oriflamme of Western civilization, the silk top hat.

Ships filled with Chinese laborers continued to arrive at San Francisco long after the completion of the Pacific Railroad where they were first used. Other railroad projects and the need for cheap labor everywhere caused a brisk demand for their service.

Age-old superstitions survived in the Chinese consciousness long after arriving in San Francisco. This man in a narrow alley regarded Arnold Genthe's camera as the evil eye and took precautions accordingly.

One of the persistent legends of San Francisco's Chinatown maintained that the real Chinese community flourished almost completely underground in a hidden city from five to eight stories deep, according to the teller. Charles Caldwell Dobie, one of the town's affectionate biographers, took a dim view of the eight story myth, but allowed that everything credited to these secret precincts went on above ground or at least no more than a single basement down. "In the sixties, seventies, eighties, nay, past even the glamorous nineties, Mongolians did flee the law, and maintain opium dens and play fan-tan and hide slave girls and engage in gangster warfare when Chicago was in its swaddling clothes ... Occasionally the white government tried to interfere. Raiding squads from police headquarters swept through Chinatown battering doors, holding suspects, rounding up witnesses. In the end it came to nothing." On this page is shown the police department's Chinatown squad in 1898 including Wong Tying, its interpreter, together with some seized opium layouts. The drawing on the page opposite appeared in *Harper's Weekly* with the chilling title: "The Haunt of the Highbinders."

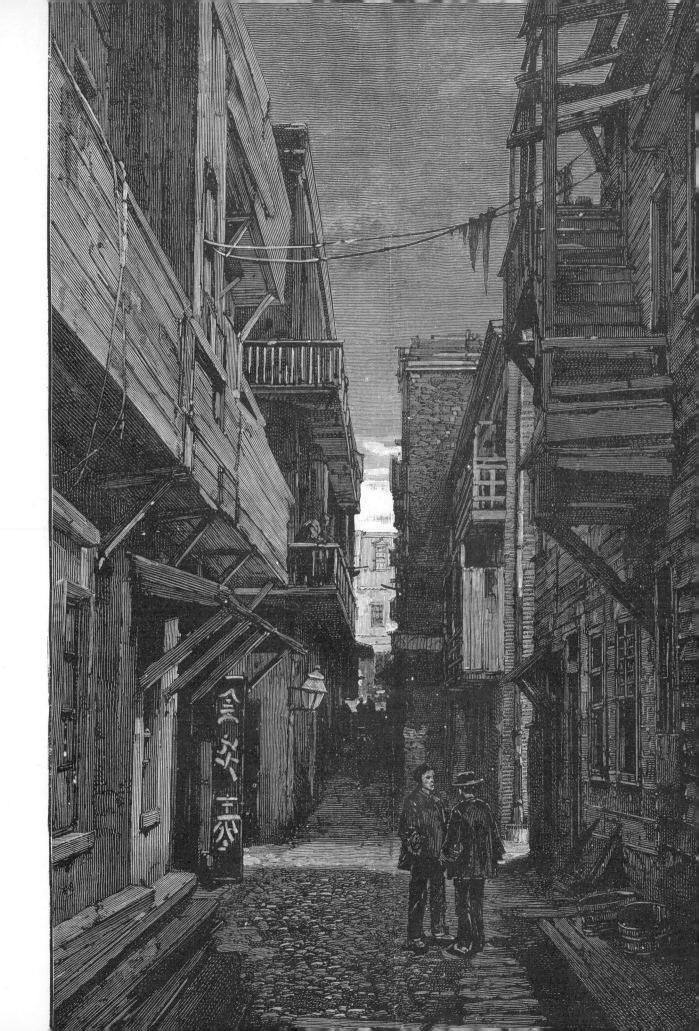

NEVADA WAGON.

AMERICAN BUGGY.

RUSSIAN SLEIGH.

RUSSIAN TROTTING WAGON.

ORIG. FARM WAGON.

PACIFIC

RUSSIAN PHAETON.

AMERICAN ROCKAWAY.

LONDON BROUGHAM.

SULKY.

STANHOPE GIG.

NORWEGIAN KARIOL.

LE GAIE QUEBEC.

BREWSTER'S CANADIAN SLEIGH.

STANHOPE PHAETON.

SKELETON WAGON.

AUSTRIAN SAND RUNNER.

CANOE-SHAPED LANDAU.

SIDE-BAR WAGON.

DOUBLE SUSPENSION VICTORIA.

Despite its multiplicity of steep hills which made driving hazardous, San Francisco was celebrated as a metropolis where horses of the well-to-do were better housed than many humans and the turnouts were the finest money could buy. The private stables of such nabobs as James Ben Ali Haggin and William Ralston were among the sights of the town and although the carriages of Comstock millionaire James Flood, reputedly the finest in the West, came from carriagemakers in London, many of the town's handsomest landaus, stanhopes and broughams came from the artisans of the Pacific Carriage Works shown here. In the sixties, boneshakers such as those depicted below, might be good for the liver but not favored by the upper classes.

By the mid-sixties San Francisco, in common with most other progressive American cities, was exchanging its omnibuses for horsecar lines which ranged in an amazement of switches, turnouts, passing tracks and turntables wherever grades permitted and traffic warranted. On the page opposite is shown a fine profile of a car and its occupants on the Market Street line that ran as far as Woodward's Gardens, and above it evidence of the overcrowding of the cars which was a perennial inspiration to artists of the time and letter writers to the editor. On this page is shown an innovation that was unique in San Francisco, a so-called balloon car devised by Henry Casebolt with a body that could be turned at the end of the run on trucks that remained placed on the tracks. The idea was to save turning on a table, but the operation involved was fully as complicated and Casebolt made no fortune from his invention.

203

The What Cheer House, no rival to The Palace but a favorite with out of town visitors who required solid comfort, was the basis of the substantial fortune with which Robert B. Woodward built Woodward's Gardens that were to be one of the city's pleasant institutions for many years. The What Cheer provided such homey comforts as open fireplaces in public rooms, a thoughtfully selected library for its guests and the first à la carte restaurant service in San Francisco. Until Woodward departed from the rule, meals had been strictly table d'hôte with no choice of dishes so far as the customer was concerned. Much was paid for that wasn't eaten. The What Cheer supplied only what was ordered and the money rolled in to make Woodward one of the town's first public benefactors and one very much appreciated.

In 1865 South Park, a faubourg of fashion and first families, was served by a horse car line connecting with North Beach. Situated between Third and Second, Bryant and Brannan Streets, South Park was a stately real estate development launched by an Englishman, George Gordon, and for several decades it boasted the residences of the Lloyd Tevises, James Ben Ali Haggins and Thomas Selbys until Nob Hill lured wealth and fashion away from Rincon Hill.

As everywhere that public conveyances ran, San Francisco's overcrowded horsecars attracted the attention of regional cartoonists.

THE CABLES

Trademark and oriflamme of San Francisco's highly individual personality for close to ninety years have been its cable cars, diminutive trams whose motive power is supplied by a patent grip alternately holding and releasing a continuously moving underground steel cable. Power to activate the more than mile-long strands of cable is supplied by huge drums at strategically located power houses and it is held or released by a functionary stationed in the forward part of the car and known as a gripman. Cable cars were invented to provide transport up the slope of San Francisco's hills, whose abrupt grades were impervious to more conventionalized forms of public carriers, and came into being in 1873 as the invention of a Scotsman named Andrew Hallidie. Motivated by humanitarian instincts which were revolted by attempts to beat horses up the hills, Hallidie built a sample length of track complete with cable and a prototypal tram up the middle of Clay Street and himself activated the grip on the first, perilous trip. The arrangement was a resounding success and one of the first revenue patrons was Fire Chief David Scannell, a professional first citizen of great daring and determination. From that day on the cable car was the symbol of San Francisco and shortly was in operation in a variety of designs including open and closed cars, dummies to accommodate crew and pilot and trailers whose only function was to cling to the rails. They were gay with scrollwork, gold trim, ornate glass transoms and maroon and cream paint and gave transport a panache of style not to be encountered in less favored communities. They ran everywhere from the Ferry Building to the Cliff House and from South Park to the Presidio. They made pots of money for their backers, the primeval Clay Street line netting sixty per cent the first year. In short, the cable car was institutional and an integral part of the fabric of the town's being that survived the fire of 1906 and for some years the competition of the automobile. They approach their tenth decade in abated dimension, but the clacking of the cables in their slots beneath the streets of the sleeping city is still the most characteristic sound of a metropolis that has come a long way since Andrew Hallidie.

The iconography of San Francisco's cable cars is almost inexhaustable. A single example will suffice here: the Clay Street line four years after its foundation with a full complement of dummy, trailer and passengers in the attire of the year 1877.

No more democratic agency of public transportation ever existed than the San Francisco cable car in the closing decades of the nineteenth century. The square derby hat of the prosperous merchant, the shawl of a market-bound housewife, the paddock coat of the sport and the widow's bonnet of ultimate respectability all are visible here in a single loading of the Clay Street cars in the years when Chester A. Arthur, "Our Chet" was in the White House.

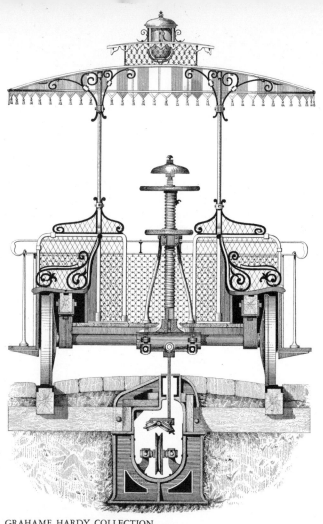

The mechanical anatomy of the cable car with its recessed slot for the activating cable and patent grip for making the car adhere to it is suggested in the sketch at the left. Below, the attire of patrons both masculine and feminine of the Sutter Street dummy and trailer suggests the mid-nineties when it was taken. In the background an egg *shampo*, a treatment for the scalp that enjoyed a universal vogue at the time, is another clue to the age with its going price of four bits.

GRAHAME HARDY COLLECTION

Believed by students of transportation to be unique in the annals of
street railways was the attempt made in San Francisco in 1863 to
convert a conventional horse-drawn street omnibus into a horsecar.
This handsome conveyance boasted a curved clerestory roof with side
transoms and arched Gothic windows ornamented with art glass. It
was the only one of its kind. Perhaps the most stylish carbarn in the
record, the structure housing this nonesuch among public conveyances
was the same Union Hall, scene of earlier civic sarabands which is
depicted in a nocturnal oil painting elsewhere in this volume. On the
page opposite the Sutter Street cable with ornate dummy and trailer
pauses for its photograph in front of Temple Emanu-El on whose site
the Medical Building at 450 Sutter stands today.

Ever aware of the enchantments that beckoned at the end of the line, San Franciscans in the nineteenth century as their successors were to do in a gasoline age, admired to journey as far as the cars would take them in search of the relaxed moments to which an industrious people were entitled. Here, in the sixties is the end of the Potrero Avenue horse car line with a crowd of interested spectators gathered for the event its arrival represented. Above on the page opposite was Dick's Saloon & Restaurant at The Beach where Willows and Wieland's Lager was available and the management posed in attitudes of smugness characteristic of saloon proprietors everywhere for a formal portrait. Below it is evidence that a progressive generation was able to achieve the Cliff House through the agency of steam as well as via bicycle and private carriage.

THREE PHOTOS: SOCIETY OF CALIFORNIA PIONEERS

A mellower time of public transportation in San Francisco is represented by the pictures on these two pages taken in an age innocent of internal combustion and still mercifully remote from jet propulsion. On the page opposite is the omnibus of the Winchester House which met the ferries connecting with transcontinental trains at Oakland and below it a special chartered by a fraternal group in 1875 posed at the Southern Pacific's modest depot at Belmont. Fourteen daycoaches for the celebrants, a baggage car for the beer and a fine, handsomely maintained American Standard locomotive on the head end; that was really living! On this page is a conversion job which transformed a car built for cable use on Page Street into an electric trolley of the Metropolitan Railway Company. Although its controls and general facade suggested those of San Francisco's classic cables, it never ran save under electric power and had control stations at both its open ends.

Cyclists in Golden Gate Park the year Dewey took
Manila *(below)* wore split skirts and knickerbockers
to be in the mode. At the right a dedicated sport in
the most approved attire had himself posed in a photographer's rainstorm just as, seventy odd years later,
a proud owner would pose in his Bugatti in the fear-
ful and wonderful garments of another age.

In 1897 the Wheelman's Rest at The Beach showed its progressive spirit by advertising a public telephone. In the below photograph the Bay City Wheelman posed in 1890 in Twenty-first Street on the eve of their Century Run in a variety of costumes that would have given pause to sports car *aficionados* in a later age.

Following the custom in older established cities such as New York and Philadelphia, San Francisco's beaux made a polite round of New Year's Day calls, sometimes ending the afternoon a little the worse for hospitality. In the nineties, Nicoll the Tailor between Third and Fourth in Market made bespoke garments for a conservative element of business men.

An authentic Beau Brummel of the Montgomery Street sixties wore a black silk frock coat with cloth buttons, a checked waistcoat and watch secured by a heavy gold Albert watch chain, a boiled shirt, stock collar and a satin bow tie of liberal dimensions. On his knee he balanced a white top hat which might change to black with the seasons and thus attired he was fit company for the other bloods of the town at the Lick House bar.

Many of the finest for-hire rigs that paraded in Golden Gate Park in the eighties came from the livery stable of J.Tompkinson on Minna Street.

In 1885 the Francis Scott Key Memorial provided a fine background for youthful fashions while the drive in Golden Gate Park attracted fashionable turnouts on a Saturday afternoon.

The distinguished newspaper artist Paul Frenzeny was so fetched by Chinese ritual that he drew this sketch of a Celestial funeral at Lone Mountain in the mid-seventies with all its symbolism and pomp of propitiatory offerings.

As stylish a funeral as the most exacting San Franciscan could ask with pompoms on a glass windowed hearse could be furnished in the sixties by Nathaniel Grey, still in business as the town's oldest firm of undertakers, or a nice last ride could be had in a railway funeral car on the proverbial one way trip to Cypress Lawn.

San Francisco's civic pride, always a sentiment of formidable dimensions which, in a later generation, was to express itself in massive devotion to art exhibits and the starchiest opera in the world, before the fire was equitably divided between the town's public wonderments and its private resources of aristocratic *ton*. Focus of its moments of public grandeur, and one that survived 1906 right into the Sheraton era, was The Palace, a corner of whose pillared Great Court is shown here. Private splendor was suggested by the drawing room of Claus Spreckels, whose French chateau on Van Ness boasted Algerian marbles, gold plated faucets and other plumbing, frescoed ceilings and rosewood, mahogany and tapestries to have pleasured a Venetian doge.

POMP & CIRCUMSTANCE

In February of 1854, three hundred of the first citizens of San Francisco foregathered at the Oriental Hotel at a dinner to celebrate the laying of municipal gas and the hotel itself blazed with the fine, new illumination. Three miles of pipe had been laid and eighty-four street lamps emplaced. As Mayor William K. Garrison arose to do the honors every light in the hotel went out, the practical joke of some wag who knew where the main intake was located. This contemporary drawing shows the mayor in full flight of forensic fancy after light and order had been restored.

Well aware from the very beginning that they were marked by destiny, the pioneers and Argonauts set about banding themselves into social groups, confraternities and organizations within a few months of their first arrival in 1849. Not only did they foregather in the name of fellowship and oratory in San Francisco itself, but groups of alumni held meetings as far abroad as New York City. Here on September 24, 1869, two hundred members of the California Pioneers Association registered at the Astor Hotel in Lower Broadway for two days of mutual congratulations on being specially favored of heaven as founders of the destinies of The Golden State.

A never ending source of civic pride and admiration in the years before The Fire were San Francisco's homes of the well-to-do which frequently received national attention for their spaciousness, cost and resources of opulent decor. On this page is a view of Linden Towers, built at San Mateo by open-handed Jim Flood, once a partner in the Auction Lunch Saloon and later one of the Big Four kings of the Comstock bonanzas. Contemporary San Franciscans smilingly called it "Flood's Wedding Cake." On the top of the page opposite is an interior of Flood's neighbor at Millbrae, Darius Ogden Mills' palatial country seat. Mills eventually took his Bank of California fortune with him to New York but members of the Mills and Reid families, with whom the Mills intermarried, used it at intervals until comparatively recent years. Below, the interior of James Ben Ali Haggin's Nob Hill palace was remarkable even in an age of elegant ostentation for its baronial magnificence.

One of San Francisco's great magnificoes of the mid-nineteenth century was Milton S. Latham, railroad builder among the redwoods and one of the big spenders on whom the town looked with awe and admiration. In 1860 Latham was inaugurated as Governor of California and three days later was designated United States Senator to replace David Broderick, killed in the infamous duel with Judge Terry. To match his senatorial status Latham built a splendid town house at the foot of Rincon Hill and an even more magnificent country seat known as *Sherwood Hall* at Menlo Park. His every property was the finest that money could buy including horses and carriages, rich household furnishings of every description and a private car on his railroad drawn by its own special engine with Latham's name in silver on the cab panel. The two interiors of *Sherwood Hall* shown on these pages suggest how a rich millionaire lived in San Francisco's golden era when money talked in loud, imperative tones for all to hear.

TWO PHOTOS: SOCIETY OF CALIFORNIA PIONEERS

The well bred family depicted in this period-piece photograph of the seventies shows the wife, domestics and children of Senator Milton S. Latham in relaxed attitudes on the lawn of *Sherwood Hall,* the baronial Latham seat at Menlo Park. Gertrude Atherton in her "Adventures of a Novelist" tells how Mrs. Latham ordered her gowns from Worth in Paris, not once a year as was the habit of most San Francisco women of fashion, but twice. Californians also were delighted with the anecdote which concerned a Nob Hill millionaire who caused to be imported at great cost a massive silver and crystal chandelier as one of the conversation pieces of his mansion only to discover it was the exact duplicate of one in the Latham stables at *Sherwood Hall.*

Senator Milton S. Latham's stables at his palatial *Sherwood Hall* at Menlo Park, shown on the page opposite, were one of the sights of the Peninsula in a time and place where stables were accounted as important as residences and almost as much money lavished on them as on the baronial mansions of the nabobs. Below is a selection of the Latham traps, pony carts, gigs, coaches and a Beverly wagon while above are shown the stalls whose chains and symbolic horse's heads were of solid silver as were the gas lighting fixtures overhead. On this page a scrupulously maintained station cart meets a group of commuters at the Southern Pacific depot at Burlingame. The year is 1899 and the train on which they rode down from the city was the *Del Monte Express* which paused briefly at Burlingame and San Jose on its fast run to Monterey with weekenders bound for Del Monte Lodge.

Perpetual darling of San Francisco's gilded age was Lillie Hitchcock Coit whose enduring memorial is the Coit Tower which overlooks the city today. In an age when the conduct of females was circumscribed by austere convention, Lillie was the town tomboy in the grand manner who attended cockfights, shaved her head to accommodate a succession of outrageous wigs, rode astride in an age which considered a sidesaddle daring and elevated herself to conspicuous estate as the official mascot of the San Francisco Fire department. Early in the fifties she became associated with Knickerbocker Engine No. 5, following it to all conflagrations, cheering its members to deeds of daring and even to the extinguishing of fires. Lillie is shown above as she was portrayed in a national magazine posed as the heroine of the hook and ladders. Below, she returns from a tour of the town's night spots, known to San Franciscans as "seeing the elephant," during which she was known to look upon the wine when it was red and be helped home in masculine attire.

By the late seventies the Amoskeag steamer had arrived but old timers remembered the volunteer companies like *Eureka* with nostalgia.

Unquestioned social leader among San Francisco's really rich millionaires was Mrs. Charles Crocker, wife of the most energetic of the Big Four builders of the Central Pacific Railroad. She ruled grandly from a $2,300,000 palace occupying the entire block on Nob Hill bounded by California, Jones, Sacramento and Taylor Streets, entertained at stunning receptions and dinners and traveled to the East aboard the Crocker private car *Mishawaka*. Of all the railroad rajahs, San Francisco liked and admired the Crockers the most as being fun people and the city's most magnificent unofficial ambassadors to the world at large.

As the Crocker mansion rose to completion as San Francisco's most fabulous residence, an undertaker named Yung who owned a forty front foot lot on the Sacramento Street side of the block it occupied attempted to hold the railroad king up for an exorbitant sum when Crocker wanted to buy him out. Rather than put up with extortion, Crocker had erected a spite fence so high that only the gables of the miserable Yung's home showed above it. The town's most sensational spite fence shows in this contemporary photograph towering higher than the roof of Crocker's neighbor, Collis Huntington in the foreground. In time Yung gave up and Crocker purchased the property at a reasonable valuation.

A day marked with a star in the annals of San Francisco was when it turned out with public ceremony and private ostentation to show General Ulysses S. Grant, newly returned from a trip around the world, what true Western hospitality meant. Thousands awaited the arrival through the Golden Gate of the steam *City of Tokio* (*below*) with the hero on board and other and, if possible, noisier thousands escorted his chariot drawn by six matched steeds to the Great Court of The Palace, as depicted elsewhere in this book. Civic receptions and municipal sarabands increased in tempo and time passed. One evening the General was the guest of honor at a private dinner given by Senator William Sharon at his magnificent estate at Belmont as shown at the top of the opposite page. On another there was a splendid illumination with fireworks (*below*) on the sand lots where only recently Dennis Kearny, the town's perpetual agitator and nuisance, had threatened to burn Grant in effigy for some now forgotten affront. In the Grant ovation, San Francisco twined threads of gold and silver in a pattern of affluence that impressed even General Grant, a man who took money seriously and was notably respectful in its presence.

Although San Francisco was not depopulated as it had been by the gold rush to the Mother Lode or, to a lesser degree, the later rush to the Comstock, its civic pulses were nonetheless fluttered excitedly by the Yukon gold rush of 1898. Overnight San Francisco became the great entrepot for Alaska, the port of entry for ships laden with the first eye-popping recoveries in gold and bullion and the point of departure for thousands of adventurers who took train and ship to the Northland. The Argonauts of 1898 ranged from skid road loungers to such socially irreproachable Nob Hill habitues as Wilson and Addison Mizner. Notable among the emigrants to the new bonanzas were scores of denizens of the Barbary Coast, gamblers, pimps, thimble riggers, green good artists, con game promoters and madames and their stock in trade, the girls. Here a group of occupants of Dawson's more stylish cribs all of them recruited from San Francisco and known, as they were christened by Jackson Chesterfield Hines, "Sweet Singer of the Yukon," as "The Pacific Street Alumni Association," pose for their photograph in a moment of relaxation. Many of the town's Cyprians achieved in Nome and Dawson City the ambition of their profession, a husband and respectability, and returned to a life of irreproachable domesticity in San Francisco after the excitements were over.

All routes by land were swamped with Yukon-bound adventurers and this contemporary photograph shows the interior of a Pullman sleeping car filled with adventurers on their way to the gold fields. Luncheon for the prudent folk in the foreground was bread and cheese; the sporting element in the rear, including Fred the inevitable porter, were more interested in bottled goods.

A popular stereoscope picture of 1898 in the sentimental spirit of the age affected to represent "The Dying Klondiker." Actually it was photographed in a San Francisco studio against a stage background with a sleeping bag borrowed from a sporting goods house. No matter. Everyone got in on the gold rush whose principal concern was with the precious metal that had always been closest to San Francisco's heart.

Market Street in 1905 was one of the famed thoroughfares of the world, ranking in celebrity with Broadway, The Strand, and Avenue de l' Opera elsewhere. The main artery of the town's retail business, its horse drawn traffic was considered formidable at the time. In the middle of the block between Third and Fourth Streets was located San Francisco's first moving picture theater, The Cinograph, admission ten cents. Further down with the white facade was the Midway Plaisance, notorious as a premises where Little Egypt, fresh from her scandalous triumph at the Chicago Fair of 1893, had danced the Dance of the Seven Veils. Youths below the age of consent were strictly barred from the Midway. In the near foreground was Goldstein, the theatrical and fancy dress costume rental man, still in business in Market Street fifty-five years later. At Shreve & Barber, the sporting goods store, you could buy a Young America double action bulldog revolver for $2.75 or a good shotgun for $8.50.

In 1905 a lone automobile in Bush Street with the Mills Building for background is parked on the left of the street against a fireplug, symbol of carefree days in downtown traffic.

Newman's Richelieu Cafe at the corner of Market and Geary courted arrest by periodically blocking pedestrian traffic with beer barrels. "Newman a Nuisance Again" in the papers he regarded as priceless publicity. Newman's annual dinner for the newsboys of San Francisco was institutional.

The hot summer noontide of a tranquil city at peace with itself and with destiny, or so it thought, was reflected in this vignette of life in Noe Street in 1906. Here the deliverymen for the San Carlos Dairy posed with their horses and express wagons before setting out on their routes. In an age innocent of more sophisticated refrigeration, their milk cans were covered with wet carpeting to keep them cool.

The last President of the United States to see San Francisco as it had been, in spirit and to a great degree in substance, since the years of gold and silver was Theodore Roosevelt who visited it during his comprehensive Western tour in 1905. No automobile marred the fine civic movement of his arrival in a state landau. Top hat and satin faced frock coat identified citizens of substance in his entourage, the police both mounted and on foot wore the helmets of respectable tradition, the slots and rails of the cable cars traced the principal thoroughfares in the pattern that was the city's inescapable hallmark. No Bulwar-Lytton was present to remark that the last days of Pompeii had been spent in similar municipal relaxation and communal rejoicing. Only in the deep waters off Point Reyes the San Andreas fault bided its time and President Roosevelt went on to the public luncheon in his honor at The Palace.

History seldom lends itself to precise compartmentation, to eras nicely definable in terms of days and hours. The decline of the Roman Empire occupied five centuries. The age named for Victoria the Good serenely survived her passing to overflow in appreciable measure into the reign of Wayward Edward. But the end of the Golden Era of San Francisco can be pinpointed in history to the day, the hour and the minute and, like everything else in the San Francisco legend it was dramatic, well defined and its consequences irrevocable. The years of the ortolans beside the Golden Gate, the times of teem and cloudy trophies on the summer horizon, the days of gold and grandeur all terminated with a definitive bang, both literally and metaphorically. The time was twelve minutes past five, give or take a few seconds, April 18, 1906 by the Christian calendar. Nothing after that moment in San Francisco was ever the same as it had been before. The thousands of clocks that were stilled by the shock were more than mere testimony to the intensity of an earthquake; they were symbols of the end of an age as clearly and abruptly separated from that which was to follow as is light from darkness. Gone in a single watch in the night was the long look of history under Spaniards to whom time meant nothing, the brave traffickings of the '49ers and the Argonauts, the massive splendors of the richest city in the world throughout decades that were in fact a torrent of wealth. And when, after days, the smoke cleared, "the damnedest finest ruins" of the City That Was were more than shattered masonry and atomized faubourgs, they were monuments to the Western way of life that was gone, now, forever. Nor will they return, for the dead return not, but must live forever in perpetual inventory of remembered things.

INDEX